Bhagwan Swaminarayan

Life and Work

Text: Sadhu Vivekjivandas

Paintings: Vasudeo Kamath

SWAMINARAYAN AKSHARPITH

1st Edition: October 2005

ISBN: 81-7526-322-9

Copies: 5,000
Rs: 125/-00

Printed & Published by:
Swaminarayan Aksharpith
Shahibaug Road,
Amdavad-4
Gujarat, India.

Websites: www.swaminarayan.org
kids.swaminarayan.org
www.mandir.org
www.akshardham.com

Preface

Yadā yadā hi dharmasya glanir bhavati Bhārat, Abhyutthānam adharmasya tadā ātmānam srujāmy aham.

O Bharat (Arjun), whenever there is a decline in dharma and a rise in *adharma*, then do I manifest.

Bhagvad Gita: 4.8.

Ever since the dawn of civilisation, the human experience of life has been defined by fluctuations between good and evil, happiness and misery, and pleasure and pain. The cause lies with man's ego and base nature, so deeply entrenched in his soul. Sometimes the consequences of turmoil and unrighteousness, due to this ignorance, are so perilous that man cannot resolve them. It is during these periods of grave crises and conflicts that God, out of his supreme compassion and grace, descends on earth to set things right. The very fact that Bhagwan Ram, Krishna and other avatars were successful in re-establishing dharma reflects that they were no mere humans, but divine beings. Therefore, we need God to liberate us from our personal miseries and the global problems that finally affect us as individuals and the nations.

Bhagwan Swaminarayan took birth during one such dark period of 18th century India, to rectify the evils that beset society. His mission was to establish Ekantik Dharma – dharma, *gnan, vairagya* and bhakti – and grant final liberation to countless souls. To fulfil this objective he left home at the age of eleven, travelled the length and breadth of India for seven years and spent the remaining thirty years of his life reforming and serving society in Gujarat.

His inspiring life and work is succinctly captured in this book, *Bhagwan Swaminarayan,* through the blessings of HDH Pramukh Swami Maharaj. Each painting and script, thirty-nine in all, describes the salient features of his extraordinary life and message. Every story unfolds the different facets of his divine personality.

We express our deep appreciations to Sadhu Ishwarcharandas and Sadhu Aksharvatsaldas for selecting the stories, Vasudeo Kamath for the wonderful paintings, Sadhu Vivekjivandas for the script, Sadhu Shrijiswarupdas for the layout and the efforts of Sadhu Amrutvijaydas and Shri Varanasi Rama Murthy for reviewing the script, and to all who have helped in making this publication possible.

— **Swaminarayan Aksharpith**

INTRODUCTION

He was a spiritual colossus who travelled barefooted across the length and breadth of India in seven years. Hailed as an unremitting champion of peace and purity, he crusaded against the crippling evils of society. Thousands admired him, obeyed him, and above all, held him in high esteem and revered him.

His name was Bhagwan Swaminarayan. He was born on 3 April 1781 in the village of Chhapaiya, near Ayodhya. He was called Ghanshyam in his childhood years. His birth was a blessed light that had dawned on earth. At the age of eight, Ghanshyam was given the sacred thread. Extraordinarily brilliant and intelligent, he completed the study of Sanskrit Grammar, the Vedas, Upanishads, Bhagvad Gita, Dharmashastras, Puranas, and Shad-Darshanas within three years. He left home at the tender age of 11 to redeem mankind.

His spiritual travels took him from Kailas-Mansarovar in the Himalayas in the north to Rameshwar in the south; and Dwarika and Somnath in the west to the Kamakshi mandir and Ganga Sagar in the east. At the time of Nilkanth's spiritual travels Sanatan Dharma was facing assaults from many imposters posing as spiritual leaders. He was thoroughly dissatisfied with the ignorance and malpractices of some priests who he came across in the course of his journey. Nilkanth encountered these masters of black magic at several places. At Kamakshi in Assam, Pibek evoked all his tantric powers to destroy Nilkanth; but he failed and was transformed. At Jagannath Puri the chief of the fake sadhus very nearly killed him. Nilkanth's intention was to inspire people lead virtuous and purposeful lives according to the tenets of dharma by freeing them from the clutches of these charlatans.

But what were the resources the young Brahmachari had at his command? His chief asset was his pure, supreme divinity that reflected his resplendent personality and serene face to the wide range of people he met during his pilgrimage.

Maharaja Ranjit Sinh, the doughty Sikh ruler who carved a niche for himself in the annals of Punjab history, was impressed with Nilkanth and sought his refuge on meeting him at Badrinath and Haridwar. The king and queen of Butolnagar in Nepal offered their daughters and their kingdom. The mahant of Shripur mandir proposed that he become the head of the mandir and manage its hefty annual income. He was greatly impressed by Nilkanth's feat when he tamed a ferocious lion. The young Brahmachari declined all offers with a smile. His mission was not to rule kingdoms, ashrams or be honoured with fame and riches.

Wherever he travelled, Nilkanth asked five questions regarding the nature of *jiva, ishwar,* maya, Brahma and Parabrahma. He did not get satisfactory replies to these questions till he reached Ramanand Swami's ashram at Loj in Saurashtra (Gujarat). With Ramanand Swami away on tour in the Kutch region, Muktanand Swami satisfactorily answered his questions. Nilkanth was pleased and decided to stay there.

In the ashram, Varni disliked the free mixing of the sexes and arranged separate discourses for men and women. Once he saw a window in the wall through which the neighbour's wife was passing on fire to a sadhu. Nilkanth saw this as a breach of dharma. He had the opening closed.

Ramanand Swami knew of Nilkanth's divinity and told his followers that he himself was merely a drum-beater and the chief player was

Varni. Ramanand Swami gave *diksha* to Nilkanth and named him as Sahajanand Swami and Narayan Muni. A year later he handed over the reins of the fellowship to Sahajanand Swami, who was only 21 years old. After Ramanand Swami passed away Sahajanand Swami gave the Swaminarayan *mahamantra* to the congregation. Thereafter he became popularly known as Bhagwan Swaminarayan.

From the age of 21 to 49, he introduced a moral, social and spiritual renaissance with the help of 3,000 *paramhansas* and sadhus that he had initiated. He exhorted people to lead a life of character and faith in God. He asked them not to kill animals, even in *yagnas,* and to abstain from eating meat, drinking alcohol and addictions.

He was against the prevailing rigidity in the caste system and opposed untouchability. He championed the welfare of women and abolished evil practices like sati and female infanticide. He succeeded in transforming lawless people like Joban Pagi, Sagram Vaghri and others into great devotees. He had a following of two million devotees, and was hailed as a torch-bearer of Indian culture.

Bhagwan Swaminarayan wrote the Shikshapatri in Sanskrit, which is a code of conduct for renunciants and householders. The Vachanamrut is a compilation of his spiritual discourses by four *paramhansas.*

The worship of Bhagwan Swaminarayan and Aksharbrahma Gunatitanand Swami, his choicest disciple and first successor, is the lynchpin of the Swaminarayan philosophy. Subsequently, the gurus who have followed in the Swaminarayan Sampraday have continued the work of Bhagwan Swaminarayan. The first guru was Aksharbrahma Gunatitanand Swami. He was succeeded by Bhagatji Maharaj, Shastriji Maharaj, Yogiji Maharaj, and the present guru is Pramukh Swami Maharaj.

In 1907, in accordance with the Vedic preachings of Bhagwan Swaminarayan, Brahmaswarup Shastriji Maharaj established the Bochasanwasi Shri Akshar Purushottam Swaminarayan Sanstha (BAPS).

As the Sampraday believes in Ekantik Bhakti and God with a form, several mandirs were built to spread bhakti and *upasana.* Bhagwan Swaminarayan had himself built six mandirs. Shastriji Maharaj built five mandirs and consecrated the *murtis* of Bhagwan Swaminarayan and Aksharbrahma Gunatitanand Swami (Akshar Purushottam Maharaj). He was succeeded by Yogiji Maharaj who spread the Satsang to East Africa and England. The present leader, Pramukh Swami Maharaj, has made the BAPS into a worldwide socio-spiritual organisation, personally inspiring and consecrating over 650 mandirs. The Akshardham monuments at New Delhi and in Gandhinagar, Gujarat, epitomise the glory of Indian culture, values and principles for the uplift of mankind. The traditional *shikharbaddh* mandirs in London, Chicago and Houston have evoked worldwide attention.

To pay tribute to Nilkanth's epic travels, Pramukh Swami Maharaj has inspired a wonderful Imax film on Nilkanth's pilgrimage at the Swaminarayan Akshardham in New Delhi. The entire complex pays obeisance to over 10,000 years of India's glorious culture, art, architecture and wisdom.

CONTENTS

iii
Preface

iv
Introduction

1
Birth

3
Death of Kalidatt

5
Transforming a Fisherman

9
Daily Routine

11
The Debate in Kashi

13
Leaving Home

17
Taming a Lion

19
Mansarovar

23 Austerities at Pulhashram

39 Travels in South India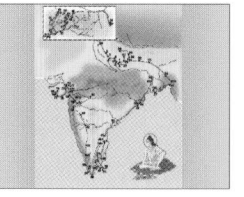

25 The Royals of Butolnagar

41 Arrival at Loj

29 Gopal Yogi

45 Plugging the Window

31 Pibek — The Tantric

47 Serving the Sick

35 Ungrateful Sevakram

49 Menial Services

51   Teaching Meditation

53   Head of Fellowship

55   Samadhi to Shitaldas

59   Five Hundred Paramhansas

61   Abolishes Sati Custom

65   No to Violent-Yagnas

67   From Dust to Gold

71   Sagram Vaghri's Hut

73   Joban Pagi

77   Diksha of Mulji Sharma

79   All Compassionate

83   "Sadguru Khele Vasant..."

87 Singers from Gwalior

89 Queen Kushalkunvarba

93 Festival of Colours

95 The Vachanamrut

97 The Shikshapatri

99 Building Mandirs

101 Meeting Sir John Malcolm

105 Love for Gunatitanand Swami

109 The Eternal Bond

110 Glossary

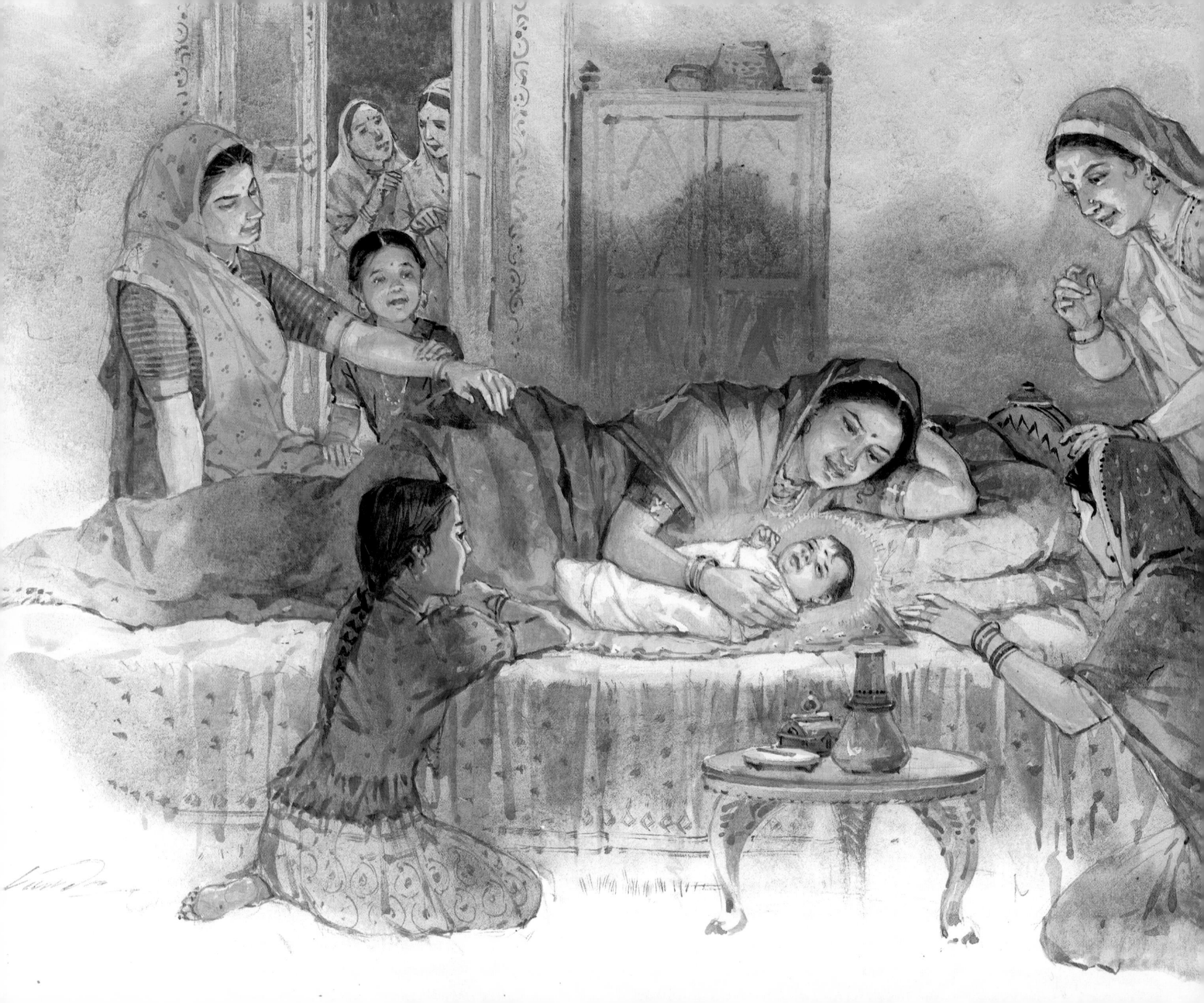

1. Birth

A small cluster of thatched, mud houses, lush farms and fields, an abundance of trees, serene lakes, cows and buffaloes grazing lazily in the morning sun, and robust men of the soil toiling in their fields and channelling water from their wells made Chhapaiya an idyllic, remote setting for an event, a celebration, the beginning of a true story that would fascinate and inspire mankind.

Chhapaiya is a tiny village near the celebrated city of Ayodhya in northern India. Dharmadev and Bhaktimata, a pious Brahmin couple, lived there. A divine prophecy was to be fulfilled through them.

It was Tuesday, 3 April 1781, (A.S. 1837, Chaitra *sud* 9). As the sun finished its daily round, night appeared dressed in all her finery, gracefully spreading across the skies, bringing with it a canopy of sparkling stars, the luminous moon, a fragrant breeze and the welcome lull after a day's toil. Nature was in its supreme elements. The house of Dharmadev and Bhaktimata was the focus of attention for the whole of Chhapaiya. Even the gods and celestial beings danced and played music in the skies to herald the advent of the newborn child. Everywhere, there was divinity, auspiciousness and unbounded joy.

At 10.00 pm the house of Dharmadev was filled with a divine glow followed by a child's cry. A beautiful baby boy was born to Bhaktimata. The villagers of Chhapaiya and the gods in the skies celebrated the event with spectacular joy and euphoria.

The womenfolk of Chhapaiya, and the friends and relatives of Bhaktimata came to see the divine child, and offered gifts and obeisance. The gods sprayed sandalwood on the house of Dharmadev. The Brahmin pundits chanted the Sam Veda mantras in sweet tones. And the growing throng outside Dharmadev's house celebrated by sprinkling the auspicious kumkum.

Bhaktimata felt blessed and tenderly embraced her child. The Brahmin pundits cast a horoscope from the presiding stars and constellations. They hailed the child as the supreme Divine entity. It was the beginning of God's prophecy that he would come in a human form to destroy evil and bless spiritual aspirants with ultimate *moksha*. Dharmadev gave donations to the Brahmins, and also generously pleased the womenfolk who had come to honour the birth of the child with gifts and wealth.

Throughout the night, Chhapaiya celebrated the advent of Ghanshyam, the supreme God.

2. Death of Kalidatt

Ever since the birth of Ghanshyam, the evil Kalidatt made several attempts to kill him.

Kalidatt was a cousin of Bhaktimata. But because of his evil nature, he treated Ghanshyam as his enemy and as a threat to his clan and sovereignty.

When Ghanshyam was an infant of six days, Kalidatt summoned a gang of demonesses by chanting a spell. Their charming looks were merely cosmetic, perfectly masking their diabolic intentions. Kalidatt ordered them to destroy Ghanshyam. The head demoness was called Kotra. She led the group to Dharmadev's house. They entered and snatched the child-God from Bhaktimata's lap, and sped off towards the forest on the outskirts of Chhapaiya. Dharmadev sent his men in pursuit but they could not catch them. On hearing Bhaktimata's heart-rending cries, Hanumanji appeared before her. On learning what had happened, Hanumanji immediately launched himself on a rescue mission. The demonesses had reached the forest and were speeding towards the den of Kalidatt. Ghanshyam's divine glance forced them to abandon him. By then Hanumanji had caught up with them and gave them a sound thrashing. The demonesses were terrified. They prayed for forgiveness and asked him to let them go. Hanumanji returned to Chhapaiya and handed Ghanshyam back to Bhaktimata.

One afternoon, when Ghanshyam was three-years-old, his friends took him to an orchard on the outskirts of Chhapaiya. Since Ghanshyam was only a child, his friends placed him under a tree while they climbed to pluck the fruits. The boys feasted upon the juicy fruits and also fed Ghanshyam. They frolicked in the serene, secluded orchard. Hours passed by in playing games. In their excitement and joy, the boys forgot all about the setting sun.

The evil Kalidatt seized the opportunity to accomplish his mission. He came and picked up Ghanshyam. Then, as he was about to smash him on the ground and kill him, Ghanshyam glanced at him. Instantly, Kalidatt felt a hot, burning sensation. He immediately released Ghanshyam and unleashed his evil powers. Kalidatt created a gust of wind. Then he covered the skies with thick, black, menacing clouds. Suddenly, there was a cloudburst and a deafening boom of thunder. Sheets of rain pounded the earth angrily. The sudden change in atmosphere frightened Ghanshyam's friends. Some froze with fear, while some took to their heels. Amidst the tempest, Ghanshyam remained unruffled.

Kalidatt then intensified the storm to uproot the mango tree under which Ghanshyam was lying. The winds wrenched the tree from its roots and crashed it upon Ghanshyam. But to Kalidatt's surprise Ghanshyam remained unscathed. He then thrust his steely arms and hands to crush Ghanshyam to death. But Ghanshyam responded with a destructive glance. Kalidatt, like a mad man, lost total control over himself. He flailed his arms and started dashing against trees till he collapsed and died.

The storm subsided. Dharmadev and the villagefolk came with oil lamps to search for Ghanshyam and his friends. When Dharmadev saw some boys frantically running towards them he enquired about Ghanshyam. "We don't know. He must be coming behind," they replied in fear and shock. Dharmadev and his party advanced, shouting Ghanshyam's name all the time. But there was no response. Finally, they entered the orchard. Soon, in the light of their oil lamps they discovered Ghanshyam playing happily with a branch beneath a mangled tree. Bhaktimata rejoiced at the sight of her lost jewel. After extricating him, Bhaktimata smothered him with love and joy. Then Dharmadev saw the body of Kalidatt which was lying in a pool of blood. Everyone heaved a sigh of relief. Ghanshyam smiled quietly in the arms of Bhaktimata. Everyone returned to the village feeling the gods had favoured them by redeeming Chhapaiya from the evil designs of Kalidatt.

3. Transforming a Fisherman

One morning Ghanshyam and his friends went for a swim in the Meen Lake in Chhapaiya. There was a large banyan tree by the lake. Ghanshyam saw a robust, dark fisherman busy catching fish in the lake. He emptied his catch into a wicker basket. The sight of dead fish made Ghanshyam unhappy. He felt sad and thought, "How could the man be so cruel and heartless by committing such a sin." His heart bled for the innocent fish. He realised that such acts were done out of ignorance of what is good and bad, truth and untruth, violence and nonviolence.

Ghanshyam resolved there and then to revive the fish. No sooner had he glanced at them again, the dead fish sprang to life. One by one they leaped into the lake. The fisherman was surprised and very angry! He tried to catch them again. But when he saw Ghanshyam looking at the fish, the fisherman was convinced that he had scuttled all his efforts. He thundered angrily, "Heh boy, why did you ruin all my efforts? I'll give you a fitting answer for your pranks." The fisherman then stormed through the waters towards the bank where Ghanshyam was standing. The other boys flinched at the fisherman's menacing strides, but Ghanshyam stood calmly. He simply glanced at the fisherman and willed that he experience the punishments of Yampuri (hell). At that very instant, the fisherman froze in his steps. Instead of Ghanshyam he saw the terrifying form of Lord Yam (the god of death). The fisherman shrieked with fear. When the servants of Lord Yam punished him mercilessly he screamed and yelled in pain and terror. He prayed to Ghanshyam for forgiveness, "O God, please save me. I will never kill fish again, nor will I ever perform any sinful acts."

Ghanshyam took pity on the repentant fisherman. His compassion had brought the dead fish back to life, and now, with the same compassion, he had reformed the fisherman. Then, on his single gesture Lord Yam and his henchmen disappeared. Once again the fisherman saw the benign form of Ghanshyam, standing by the banks. Ghanshyam advised him, "Just like you the fish, too, have the right to live!"

The fisherman promised to give up his sinful ways. He pledged never to kill fish or any other animals. His realisation of the rights and wrongs of life made him feel blessed. He bowed in reverence to Ghanshyam.

The people of Chhapaiya began to notice that Ghanshyam, who was still a child, was born with a higher mission in life.

His acts were purposeful and aimed at transforming and elevating all. Ahimsa was one of the many virtues he would establish and consolidate in the lives of countless people all through his life.

4. Daily Routine

When Ghanshyam was three years old Dharmadev and his family left Chhapaiya to live in the nearby famous city of Ayodhya. At the age of five Ghanshyam commenced his studies in Mathematics, Geography, Astronomy, History, Astrology and the Purans from his teacher, Hrudayram. Ghanshyam led an austere and simple lifestyle, practising the ideals of the *brahmacharya* ashram.

Every morning he would go for an early bath in the river Saryu. Thereafter he would visit the mandirs on his way back home. After performing his daily worship at home, Ghanshyam would study. At lunchtime he would bathe again and offer food to the *murti* of God in his home mandir. He would take a little of the sanctified food for lunch, mix it and eat sparingly. After lunch, he would take an afternoon nap, lying on the bare floor. Once, when Dharmadev told him not to sleep on the floor, Ghanshyam replied that it was necessary to be austere during his student days.

Then Dharmadev would teach him the Hindu shastras: Vedas, Upanishads, Shaddarshans, Shrimad Bhagvat, Ramayan, Mahabharat, Vasudev Mahatmya of Skand Puran, Bhagvad Gita, Vidur Niti, Yagnavalkya Smruti and other scriptures. In the evening, Ghanshyam would go again to the river Saryu for a bath and offer his evening prayers. On his way home he would visit all the mandirs for darshan, then pray and leave after the *arti*. It was a pleasant sight to see him walk through the streets of Ayodhya for his ritual holy bath in the river Saryu and doing darshan at the mandirs. People were attracted to him because of his tender age and spiritual magnetism.

Ghanshyam always visited the Hanuman Gadhi mandir. The devotees would give him passage while he was climbing, and felt blessed to see a little boy wedded to devotion. Here Ghanshyam would do darshan of the *murti* of Hanumanji and pray to him. Then he would patiently listen to the narration of the Ramayan read by the mahant of the mandir.

After returning home, Ghanshyam would have dinner and then revise the lessons he had been taught in the morning. Finally, before retiring to bed, he would chant God's name.

During his academic years, Ghanshyam remained focussed in his studies, spiritual activities and a simple lifestyle. He showed a disinterest in all worldly affairs.

5. The Debate in Kashi

When Ghanshyam was 11 years old Dharmadev took him to the famous, ancient city of scriptural learning, Kashi, to observe a lunar eclipse. Kashi is also known as Benaras or Varanasi.

During the eclipse Dharmadev, Ghanshyam and other Brahmins chanted the holy name of God on the steps of the Manikarnika Ghat. Thereafter they bathed and Dharmadev gave donations to the Brahmins. Both father and son returned to their guesthouse. As word spread the next day of Dharmadev's presence in the city Brahmin pundits came to pay their respects. In scholarly circles Dharmadev was known for his great learning. On knowing that he was going to stay for ten more days they arranged a debate at the Gomath ashram by the river Ganga. Pundits of the Shankar, Ramanuj, Madhva, Vallabh, Chaitanya and other philosophies assembled for the grand debate. Everyone was impressed on seeing the 11-year-old Ghanshyam. They were eager to hear him speak.

First, an Advait pundit stated, "Everything is Brahma (supreme being). There is nothing but Brahma. Only Brahma is real and eternal, whereas all that has name and form is illusory. So, there is no real world and the *jivas* are fundamentally Brahma."

Ghanshyam countered, saying, "Respected pundits! What you say is not true. It does not conform to the message of the shastras. Like the soul-body relationship, God is the soul and the world is its body. Since they are two different entities, you cannot say that there is only one reality called Brahma.

"Secondly, just as God is eternal, so too, are the *jivas* and *maya*. God, *jiva* and *maya* are distinct and eternal entities. But when you say that everything is Brahma and there is nothing but Brahma then where lies the distinction between the preacher and the disciple!…"

Ghanshyam's fluent and plausible explanations from the shastras stunned the pundits. The debate continued with a further argument posed by another Advait pundit, "Just as out of ignorance one perceives a snake in a rope and silver in a conch shell, so too, because of ignorance the world appears real but it is false and an illusion."

Ghanshyam smiled with confidence and replied, "Because the snake and silver truly exist, one can conceive of an illusion

of a snake and silver in a rope and conch shell respectively. If they had never existed, how could one perceive them even as an illusion?"

Ghanshyam's arguments were strong and logical. He believed that there are five eternal entities: *jiva, ishwar, maya,* Brahma and Parabrahma. God or Parabrahma is supreme. Brahma is his choicest disciple and divine abode, also called Akshar or Aksharbrahma. Brahma has form as well as formlessness. Parabrahma has a definite divine human form; he is the master, the all-doer who pervades in and controls all the four entities.

While Ghanshyam spoke all the pundits in the assembly experienced samadhi and saw in him the divine form of their own chosen deities. The bliss of seeing Shankaracharya, Shiv, Ram and Krishna overwhelmed everyone. When they came out of samadhi they spontaneously lauded him as the supreme God, "O God, you are supreme and the cause of all divine incarnations. May we be blessed with this realisation of your true form."

The pundits experienced that God's divine form was a matter of realisation rather than one of discussion and debate alone. One by one they bowed to Dharmadev and prostrated to Ghanshyam and offered him gifts.

Ghanshyam's victory filled Dharmadev's heart with pride and joy. In his happiness his son's glory flashed through his mind. But the reverie was brief, abruptly cut short by Ghanshyam's enquiry, "Father, when are we returning to Ayodhya?"

The next day Dharmadev and Ghanshyam returned to Ayodhya.

6. Leaving Home

A few months later both Bhaktimata and Dharmadev passed away. Ghanshyam had planned to leave home after redeeming his parents. Rampratapbhai, his elder brother, noticed a growing disinterest for worldly affairs in Ghanshyam's attitudes and actions. He tried to keep him happy and cheerful. Soon there were offers for his marriage. Ghanshyam flatly turned down the proposals and told Rampratapbhai that he was not interested at all. That same night Ghanshyam resolved to renounce home and set out on his spiritual mission.

It was early Friday morning 29 June 1792 (A.S. 1849, Ashadh *sud* 10). Ghanshyam woke up at 4.00 am. Everyone in the house was fast asleep. He hurriedly started preparing himself to leave home. He matted his hair into a bun, put on a loincloth and wrapped a piece of cloth over it. He wore a *kanthi* made of tulsi and placed a Shaligram for worship around his neck. Then he picked up a gourd, filter cloth, an armrest and a small book that he had prepared himself on the essence of all shastras. He was now ready to leave home. He took only the minimum of possessions for his epic pilgrimage throughout India.

Ghanshyam's divine persona cut a figure of renunciation and determination. He was only 11 years old! He looked at his family, bowed to them and then quietly stepped out of his home. It was a historic moment. A new chapter dawned in the life of the divine child-yogi of Ayodhya. He would be known as Nilkanth Varni during his travels.

The city of Ayodhya once mourned when Shri Ram left to fulfil his exile of fourteen years, but today Ghanshyam was leaving Ayodhya forever; never to return again! The ancient city lamented his departure. In the waning moonlight, Nilkanth walked through the silent streets and lanes of Ayodhya. Along his path some faint lights emerged from a few homes, only to be lost and dissolved in the inky darkness. The sweet Vedic recitations from a school of Brahmin boys wafted through the morning calm. It was a fitting tribute for his departure and an auspicious beginning to an intrepid journey. On reaching the banks of the river Saryu, Nilkanth noticed an evil man following him. In a flash the man picked up Nilkanth and threw him into the raging river to destroy him. As if to protest his heinous act the skies raged and thundered. A storm broke out. The man burst out into a sinister laughter and in the next second he lost his sanity. He crashed against a tree and died instantly.

Nilkanth swam and reached the opposite bank. He sat beneath a tree to rest. The monsoon season had set in. The sky was overcast and the air was cool and saturated with moisture. After a while Nilkanth stood up and walked fearlessly, unmindful of the denizens of the jungle. He trod the hostile land barefooted with determination, joy and freedom.

Back in Ayodhya, when Suvasini Bhabhi, Rampratapbhai found out that Ghanshyam had left, they collapsed and broke down. No amount of consolation could pacify them or make them come to terms with the reality of his departure. Both felt that Ghanshyam had left because of the proposal for his marriage. But, in reality, Ghanshyam had left to establish Ekantik Dharma for the liberation of countless souls.

7. Taming a Lion

Nilkanth Varni trekked up north passing through the towns and villages of Lodheshwar, Jetpur, Pathepur, Bareli, Haridwar and Tapovan. He preached and enlightened people along the way. He preferred to halt for the night in places of solitude. One evening, he arrived in the village of Shripur. Nilkanth went to its outskirts and settled down on a platform outside a quiet ashram. All around was a forbidding jungle, ruled by thick vegetation and ferocious animals.

The mahant of the ashram came out on seeing the illustrious Nilkanth. He was impressed with the young ascetic.

"Brahmachariji, please come inside the ashram. It is dangerous to stay here outside. Come and join us," the mahant requested as he pointed towards the ashram.

Nilkanth was deaf to the cares and concerns of the mahant.

"Brahmachari, you must be hungry. Come inside, have dinner and then rest in comfort and safety."

The mahant wondered and looked at Nilkanth. He thought he must have taken a vow of silence. So he gently shook him and told him, "Maharaj, pay heed to my words. If you do not desire to come into the ashram then please go into the village where there are people, and safety. Here, at night, there is nothing but imminent death."

"Mahantji!" Nilkanth spoke calmly. "I do not prefer to live in a populated place. Instead the village outskirts and the open skies suit me well. And, besides, I have no fear of death."

The mahant was astonished. He commented, "O young ascetic, you are stubborn. Why do you wish to die purposely?"

"Mahantji, one cannot stop death by hiding away from it. If it is ordained then it will strike anywhere – inside or outside! I appreciate your concern, but I am going to stay the night here, come what may!"

The mahant shook his head in disbelief and went inside the ashram. There was nothing he could do to save him. The sun went down and the people of Shripur locked their doors and windows. The village and the ashram wore a deserted look.

Nilkanth sat down in meditation. As the night advanced the jungle became more and more frightening. Predators of all kinds were on the prowl. After midnight a lion's roar rent the air. The people of Shripur, the mahant and his disciples were startled from their sleep. Nilkanth remained unperturbed in his meditation. The mahant feared for Nilkanth's life, as a ferocious lion came roaring out of the jungle towards him. His sheer size was overwhelming. He strode like a tyrant, programmed to kill and devour. His angry eyes flashed like burning coal and its strides shook the earth. The mahant and his disciples shuddered with fear. Nilkanth calmly opened his eyes and cast a divine glance at the lion. The lion was pacified instantly and went into samadhi. Like a lamb it came and sat at the feet of Nilkanth. The soul of the silent lion experienced bliss. Nilkanth caressed the lion's head and golden mane. The mahant opened the windows of his room with fear, expecting to find blood and gore. But he and his disciples stood transfixed in wonder. They saw the lion licking the feet of Nilkanth. His roars and snarls had turned into tender growls of joy. The mahant and his disciples looked at each other in fascination and said, "He must be an incarnation of God. He is either Shiv or Krishna!"

Nilkanth tamed the wild beast. His only desire was to redeem whoever came to him. And today it was the turn of a lion!

The night passed and morning heralded its arrival with the faint amber glow of the sun's rays filtering through the dense jungle. Nilkanth got up and walked towards the river to perform his ablutions. The lion, too, followed him. On reaching the river Nilkanth told the lion, "Now, you may go your way." Immediately, the lion bowed and walked away into the thick jungle.

The mahant and his disciples, who were observing Nilkanth from a safe distance, saw this. After he bathed, Nilkanth was performing his rituals of worship. The mahant and the people of the village came to see him and to offer their reverence to him. Nilkanth was absorbed in his morning worship. The mahant's voice resonated with adoration, "Brahmachariji, you are a great, divine person. Come and stay with us in the ashram. We shall appoint you as our head. We have an annual income of Rs. 100,000..." The mahant voiced his appreciation and request to Nilkanth.

"Look Mahantji! If I had desired for the mundane honours and positions of an ashram or institution then why would I have renounced my home! My only aim is to travel to places of pilgrimage and redeem people and show the world the true path of spirituality!"

Nilkanth concluded his worship. The mahant prayed and requested again, but Nilkanth remained unflagging in his resolve. He stood up and walked towards the thick jungle. The mahant and the people of Shripur watched him with amazement and adoration, never to forget him. Nilkanth redeemed their lives with his brief miraculous association.

8. Mansarovar

From Shripur Nilkanth Varni travelled through the bushes and forests to Guptakashi, where, ancient sages had performed austerities to please Lord Shiv thousands of years ago. From here he went to Guptaprayag which hugs the banks of the river Ganga. Nilkanth proceeded ahead to the pilgrim places of Triyugi Narayan, Gaurikund, Kedarnath and Badrinath. The priest of Badrinath Mandir was impressed by the radiant personality of Nilkanth. Everyday he served Nilkanth with food that had been offered to the deities. The priest requested Nilkanth to stay at Badrinath. Nilkanth remained quiet. It was his way of politely saying no.

When King Ranjit Sinh of Punjab came to Badrinath for darshan he was attracted by Nilkanth's divine charisma. He realised that Nilkanth was God, and Nilkanth in return promised him redemption.

After celebrating Diwali and New Year's day in Badrinath, Nilkanth decided to proceed up north towards Badrivan in the Himalayas. The priest told him not to go because of the terrible winter and barren terrain. "No human being can travel to that perilous place, and no one has ever desired to do so," the priest pleaded. But Nilkanth remained committed in his mission to go to Badrivan. Though it was October and winter time, Nilkanth did not care about the bitter challenges ahead. On the way he sanctified the icy cold waters of a lake by taking a dip. On Wednesday, 7 November 1792 (A.S. 1849, Kartak *vad* 8) he reached the ashram of Nar-Narayan Rishis in Badrivan. He was welcomed and honoured by them. Here Nilkanth performed austerities for three months for the redemption of aspirants, not eating a single morsel of food. On his departure Nilkanth blessed Nar-Narayan Rishis for serving him.

Nilkanth Varni proceeded to Mansarovar – a beautiful pristine lake near the holy mountain of Kailash: the abode of Lord Shiv. Nilkanth was only 12 years old. The bone-chilling icy winds blew along the route, at gale-force. The desolate landscape and the solitary path had no effect on Nilkanth. In fact Nilkanth travelled happily, absorbed in his own divinity. On reaching Mansarovar, he rejoiced at the sight of the transparent cobalt-blue waters of the lake. There were beautiful red lotuses and fish in the lake. By its banks trotted the legendary snow-white swans. The ambience of Mansarovar was very pleasant and divine. The air was filled with the fragrance of flowers wafted by a gentle breeze. Nilkanth was immensely pleased to be by the banks

of the holy lake.

Nilkanth took a dip in the freezing waters of Mansarovar. Then he offered fruits to the Shaligram and ate a little. For five days Nilkanth stayed there. He meditated, contemplated on his mission and blessed the white swans. He told them to come to the west where he would fulfil the devotion of his devotees and redeem them.

On Monday, 13 May 1793 (A.S. 1849, Vaishakh *sud* 3) Nilkanth returned to Badrinath. The priest welcomed him and offered him food for dinner. Nilkanth Varni was pleased by the priest's hospitality and devotion and said, "When I departed I had food here and now on my return I'll be taking food after several months."

Nilkanth Varni's austerities and pilgrimage to one of the most challenging and severest corners of the earth solely for redeeming souls and sanctifying places reflect his compassion, and transcendence to all physical hardships and fearlessness.

Mansarovar, a natural holy lake, is situated in the southwest corner of Tibet, 20 km from Mt. Kailash. It lies at a height of 4560 m and is one of the country's most sacred and beautiful lakes. The devout take a dip in the lake's icy waters and circumambulate it to wash away their sins. The 110 km circumambulatory path of the lake is sometimes sandy, gravelly and marshy. Its waters are cobalt-blue in colour and crystal clear. The high elevation lends it a radiance unmatched by other lakes. The buffeting winds and the winter chill are very severe and dangerous. May, June and September are the best months to visit. Nilkanth Varni visited Mansarovar during the harsh, frigid winter months of October and November.

9. Austerities at Pulhashram

From Badrinath Nilkanth Varni went to Haridwar and then returned to Ayodhya. From here he headed north towards Pulhashram in Muktinath, Nepal. On the way he was welcomed by the King and Queen of Vanshipur. Both of them and their daughters lovingly served Nilkanth and listened to his spiritual discourses. Then the King and Queen requested Nilkanth to marry their daughters and be the heir to their kingdom. Nilkanth refused and explained that he had a greater mission to accomplish. One quiet, early morning Nilkanth left to continue his journey.

The monsoon month of Ashadh A.S. 1850 (1793 CE) had set in. The rains were a welcome respite from the torrid summer months. Nature celebrated its monsoon hues. After one month Nilkanth entered the impenetrable forest cupped in the valley of the Black Mountain. The forest was so dense that not even a ray of light could penetrate during the day. Nilkanth walked for three days and nights undeterred by the ferocious animals. When he emerged from the forest it was Friday, 23 August 1799 (A.S. 1856, Shravan *vad* 8). One year and forty-three days had passed since he had left home. Nilkanth bathed in the river and offered fruits to his Shaligram.

Nilkanth Varni travelled by the banks of the river Kali Gandki towards Muktinath. Along the way he came across the formidable force of the river Kali Gandki flowing between the Kala Parvat and Mt. Shvetgiri. The river had carved its course through the mountains. To proceed to Muktinath there was no other way except through the river. The river was infested with poisonous snakes and crocodiles. Without a thought for his life, Nilkanth plunged into the torrent. By his wish the snakes and crocodiles were numbed into samadhi. Nilkanth waded all night through the river, reaching the other end of the mountain tunnel at dawn. After completing his morning rituals he proceeded ahead. Soon Nilkanth saw the imposing snow-capped Kala Parvat (23,698 ft) and Mt. Shvetgiri (26,811 ft). The rest of his journey to Muktinath, perched at 12,500 ft, was dangerous because of the steep ascents and descents. On arriving at Muktinath, Nilkanth was overjoyed. The panoramic view of the Himalayas was divine and majestic. Nilkanth went for darshan at the pagoda-shaped Vishnu mandir. The mandir shrine had the *murtis* of Shri Vishnu, Shridevi, Bhudevi and Garudji. Nearby was a natural reservoir of water where Bharat, son of King Rishabhdev, had performed austerities thousands of years ago. A little further down, Pulaha, the son of Brahma, had performed austerities and so the place was known as Pulhashram. Nilkanth Varni resolved to perform austerities for the liberation of aspirants.

The next day Nilkanth woke up at 4.00 am, took his bath in the icy waters of river Gandki. After having darshan at the Vishnu mandir, he came to the water reservoir where Bharat had performed austerities and stood on one leg, raised his arms upwards and started meditating. Wearing only a loincloth, Nilkanth, only 12 years old, stood deeply absorbed in meditation and austerity. His face beamed with spiritual radiance and tranquillity. The wintry chill and howling winds did not budge him one bit from his resolve.

Nilkanth chanted the Gayatri mantra (mantra to appease the Sun-god) and sometimes he recited the Sam Veda mantras. He abstained from food; taking only water or an occasional fruit. He continued his austerities in this fashion all through the night and followed the same routine every day for nearly two and a quarter months. Sometimes the priest of the Vishnu mandir and a few pilgrims who came to the mandir watched Nilkanth's austerities with fascination and awe. The priest felt Nilkanth to be a divine boy.

On Thursday, 14 November 1793 (A.S. 1850, Kartak *sud* 11) the Sun-god was pleased by Nilkanth's austerities and he appeared in his illustrious human form. Nilkanth paid his respects and prayed to bless him so that he could observe *brahmacharya* in his life. The Sun-god spoke of Nilkanth's glory as the supreme God and expressed his hesitancy in blessing him. "O Lord, I know that you desire to establish *brahmacharya* as an ideal of dharma. Because one who follows *brahmacharya* can attain the God-realised state. You are the source of all virtues, therefore, what you have asked for shall be accomplished."

Nilkanth Varni was happy at the blessings of the Sun-god and bowed to him. Soon thereafter the Sun-god disappeared. Nilkanth concluded his austerities, offered his respects at the Vishnu mandir and resumed his pilgrimage towards Nepal.

10. The Royals of Butolnagar

Nilkanth continued his trek through the mountainous terrain of Nepal. He passed through dark and dangerous forests that lay along his way. Because of his severe austerities he had become indifferent to the harsh, cold weather and torturous terrains. To advance ahead he never hesitated in plunging in rampaging rivers or swimming in water infested with snakes and crocodiles. As he walked he would sometimes sing the Bhramar Geet (from the Shrimad Bhagvad) or say the *mala*.

After some time Nilkanth arrived at an impressive city. He saw a beautiful garden by the riverside. He asked some sadhus staying there whether he could stay. "Brahmachari, this is the king's garden. He permits pilgrims to stay here and also provides meals," they replied.

"What is the name of this city?" Nilkanth asked.

"Butolnagar. King Mahadutt is the sovereign of this land," replied the sadhus.

Nilkanth thanked the sadhus and sat beneath a tree. Then King Mahadutt and his sister, Queen Maya, came to the garden to pay their daily respects to the sadhus. When they came to Nilkanth, both the king and queen stood transfixed in amazement. Nilkanth's illustrious face and divine persona was very attractive and peaceful. They realised that the Brahmachari was different from the other sadhus. Queen Maya pitied Nilkanth's emaciated body. Out of her love and concern she told him to stay in the bungalow. Nilkanth said that there was no need, and that he was happy living in the open.

"Brahmachariji, I have built these bungalows for sadhus to stay and rest. I will be blessed and redeemed if you stay in one of them," the king requested.

Nilkanth fulfilled the king's wish. King Mahadutt appointed one of his servants to look after Nilkanth's needs. Subsequently, some of the sadhus turned green with envy for the special attention the king was giving to Nilkanth.

Each morning Nilkanth would wake up early, take his bath in the river and sit beneath the tree to perform his ritual worship. The king would send a plate of food for Nilkanth at lunchtime, but Varni gave it to the sadhus and ate only fruits. When the king arrived Nilkanth would explain to him about *atma* and Paramatma. "The *atma* is different from the body. Due to body-consciousness one's devotion becomes fraught with obstacles. One should transcend the bondages of this world by

identifying one's *atma* with Brahma. Only then does one become eligible to offer the highest devotion to Parabrahma." Nilkanth also explained that *atma* is different from Paramatma and it is not a part and parcel of God.

When the king's daughter came with her friends to play in the garden their minds were pacified by Nilkanth's meditative figure. The king and queen then decided to take Nilkanth under the shelter of their palace. But Nilkanth refused. "But will you not at least come for lunch at our palace?" Queen Maya asked. Nilkanth was touched by the queen's sentiments and thus agreed.

Daily, Queen Maya devotionally prepared different food items for Nilkanth. Gradually, through their services to Nilkanth the hearts of the king and queen became pure. Soon they realised that Nilkanth was divine and none other than God himself.

Nilkanth's mission was now over. He saw that the king and queen had realised the knowledge of his divine form. So he made arrangements to leave. He tied his Shaligram around his neck and picked up his gourd and staff. As he left his room he found Queen Maya standing before him. "Brahmachariji, where are you going in this manner?" she asked. Nilkanth did not reply. At that time King Mahadutt arrived. He understood Nilkanth's intention. "Maharaj! You stayed with us for so long and blessed us with the knowledge of your divinity. And now you are ready to leave us! My children have become spiritually inclined through your company. How can we live without you!"

Again Nilkanth remained silent. On the one hand his greater mission had yet to be fulfilled and on the other was the profound devotion of King Mahadutt and Queen Maya.

"O King, it is time that I left. I have my mission to accomplish. There are many spiritual aspirants waiting for me."

But the king and queen did not allow him to leave. Nilkanth kept his meagre belongings back into the room. However, that night Nilkanth quietly left the palace. In the morning when Queen Maya found that Nilkanth had gone she ordered a detachment of cavalry to bring him back. Nilkanth was found and he returned at their requests and prayers.

Queen Maya told his brother, Mahadutt, to post his soldiers at the borders of their kingdom lest Nilkanth should slip away again. Nilkanth stayed for a few days and after celebrating the festival of Janmashtmi on Monday, 18 August 1794 (A.S. 1851) he left.

Nilkanth Varni proceeded in the northerly direction on the road to Pokhra.

11. Gopal Yogi

The path to Pokhra was strewn with hardships. Nilkanth walked through the bushes, thorns and the jungle wilderness. His brisk pace and determination was due to an inner call of a magnanimous soul in the depths of the forest. Soon, Nilkanth's inexorable march would come to an end at a beautiful hermitage. From a distance he saw an illustrious yogi lost in meditation beneath a sprawling banyan tree. His decades of spiritual endeavours were evident from his aging face, snow-white beard and matted locks. He was sitting in a yogic posture on a deer skin beneath the banyan tree. Nearby was his simple straw hut. After performing his daily worship rituals the yogi was about to read the Bhagvad Gita when he saw Nilkanth approaching. He was overwhelmed with joy because he realised that the one whom he was meditating upon had arrived in flesh and blood. He got up immediately and ran fervently towards the young Brahmachari. Nilkanth, too, ran towards the yogi. On meeting, the two embraced each other with joy. It was October 1794 (A.S. 1851 in the month of Kartak).

"O Lord, you have kept me waiting for so long!" the yogi spoke in a baritone voice.

Nilkanth smiled and replied, "I have been travelling the mountains and forests in search of a yogi like you. But nowhere have I seen a pure yogi like yourself." The yogi felt blessed on meeting Nilkanth.

Nilkanth further praised the yogi, "You must have had a great guru, without whom, you could not have mastered the art of yoga. I travelled to Badrivan but I did not find a yogi of your calibre. I wish to learn yoga from you."

Gopal Yogi was pleased by Nilkanth's presence in his ashram. He taught the yoga scriptures and various steps of Hatha Yoga. Nilkanth was quick in grasping the yogic steps of *yam, niyam, asan,* pranayam, *dharna* and dhyan. Within a short span of one year Nilkanth mastered the eight steps of *ashtang* yoga. He told Gopal Yogi, "Now I can see my own *atma*." Gopal Yogi knew that Nilkanth was God so there was no question of him having attained *atma*-realisation; in fact he was eternally realised. Then Nilkanth explained the principles of associating and identifying one's *atma* with Brahma. "The fruit of *ashtang* yoga is samadhi in which one enjoys the divine bliss of God. But this is not the ultimate state of realisation. Only when one identifies one's *atma* with Brahma does one become totally free from the fetters of maya and attain the *gunatit* state. Then one becomes eligible to offer the highest devotion to God."

Gopal Yogi had attained the state of *atma*-realisation through yoga and believed that it was the final stage of his spiritual endeavours. But through his association with Nilkanth he was blessed with the realisation of identifying his *atma* with Brahma. From thenceforth he experienced God in his own *atma* and the form of Nilkanth to be one. Gopal Yogi became free from all mundane inclinations and a few days later attained liberation in the presence of Nilkanth. Varni performed the last rites and departed in November 1795 (A.S. 1852 in the month of Kartak). He had spent one full year at the ashram of Gopal Yogi. Nilkanth resumed his journey towards Pokhra and Kathmandu.

Nilkanth continued his spiritual odyssey and reached Kathmandu in Nepal in 1796. After visiting the Pashupatinath mandir he blessed King Ranbahadur and cured him of his chronic disease. Varni forged ahead and reached Sirpur in the kingdom of King Siddhavallabh. The king hosted bands of migrant wayward sadhus that wandered into his kingdom. Nilkanth reformed the sadhus and enlightened the king about the qualities of a true sadhu.

12. Pibek — The Tantric

Next, Nilkanth travelled eastwards towards Assam, arriving at Kamakshi mandir in October 1796 (A.S. 1853, Kartak). The mandir was on top of a hill and Kamakshi Devi was the presiding deity. Nilkanth took refuge in a garden by the river Brahmaputra that flowed at the foot of the hill. A band of fake sadhus was also camping in the garden, preying upon the innocent locals and pilgrims who came for darshan of Kamakshi Devi. They extorted money with threats and demonstrations of black magic and superstition. When the locals saw Nilkanth they started gravitating towards his serene and sober presence, and assembled before him. The fake ascetics were infuriated at them for neglecting the goddess by not going for her darshan first. They were jealous of the child-yogi's magnetism. So, they instigated Pibek — a notorious tantric who worshipped the goddess Mahakali — to get rid of Nilkanth.

Pibek was formerly a pious Brahmin, but due to his association with the corrupting Kaul, Shakta and Vammargi sects he degenerated and started indulging in eating meat, drinking liquor and adultery. Then by worshipping several goddesses he attained supernatural powers, which inflated his ego. Then Pibek started exercising his powers to create a band of followers. He believed himself to be invincible.

One morning, after having darshan of the goddess, Nilkanth returned to the garden and sat beneath a tree. He began discoursing to the sadhus who had been travelling with him from Sirpur. Pibek came with his motley band of disciples to the garden. He had resolved to defeat Nilkanth and the sadhus and make them into his disciples.

On reaching Nilkanth, Pibek broke out into a diabolic laughter. The sadhus and the lay were petrified and disgusted by the sight of Pibek and his indecent disciples.

Nilkanth calmly told everyone, "Do not be afraid at all. Listen to what I am saying, and do not look at Pibek."

Pibek became uneasy at Nilkanth's equanimity. He exploded again in guffaws. The sadhus trembled at this and were getting ready to leave. Nilkanth restrained them, "Why are you going away? There is no need to be afraid of one who is so low and vile. Without God's divine powers no one can kill anyone in this universe."

Pibek roared at Nilkanth, "Boy, you are only a child! You have not seen my powers!!"

Nilkanth smiled without the slightest anxiety. The people around him advised, "Varni! This master of mantras will reduce you to ashes."

"No one other than God can command Death. If he wants to exercise his powers, then let him do so," Nilkanth replied calmly.

As a demonstration of his diabolic powers Pibek threw a handful of charmed grains on a nearby banyan tree. Instantly, the tree withered and died.

The sadhus with Nilkanth were terrified, and they started leaving. Varni reassured them, "Why are you so scared? Let him first try his mantras on me. And if anything fatal happens, then you can go."

On hearing this Pibek turned mad with rage. He rained his charmed grains on Nilkanth.

But nothing happened. This enraged him further. "Now, your death is near," he shouted.

Nilkanth smiled and said, "Do whatever you want to without talking. Even Kal Bhairav or Batuk Vir will not be able to harm me."

Pibek summoned Kal Bhairav, but he could not approach Varni. When he called Batuk Vir, he too, stood still momentarily and then pounced upon Pibek instead. His defeat infuriated him all the more. Though he was bruised and in pain because of the assault, he got up and evoked Hanumanji. When Hanumanji saw Varni, he bowed to him and pummelled Pibek with blows on his face and head. Pibek collapsed to the ground, unconscious and bleeding profusely.

The relatives of Pibek prayed to Nilkanth to have mercy upon him. When Nilkanth chanted the holy name of God in his ears, Pibek regained consciousness. He got up and bowed at Varni's feet. But the bitterness of defeat lingered on because of his punctured ego.

That night, Pibek was aroused with vengeance towards Varni. He invoked Kal Bhairav again. When he appeared, Pibek prayed, "None of my powers could defeat Varni. Now you will have to save my name."

Bhairav warned him, "Why do you still entertain the desire to kill one who is the Master of Death! If you wish to be redeemed then take his refuge. You will be saved from the cycles of birth and death."

Pibek realised his mistake. The next morning, after having his bath, he donned a pair of white clothes and went to

Nilkanth. He prostrated before Varni and cried in repentance for his misdeeds. Nilkanth said, "Pibek, one who is spiritually realised never frightens or threatens others. My powers of God have dissolved your powers of black magic."

Pibek listened in silence. His disciples wondered as to why he had turned docile. None of them could look into Varni's pure, divine eyes. Pibek's ego melted and true knowledge dawned within his heart. He saw the divine form of Bhagwan Vishnu in Nilkanth Varni.

Varni finally blessed Pibek and said, "Now tonsure your head, apply a Vaishnav *tilak* on your forehead, read the Bhagvad Gita daily and worship Bhagwan Vishnu. Do not attire yourself in a manner which frightens others. Wear ordinary, sober clothes. Do not practice black magic anymore. God will redeem you." Pibek and his disciples left feeling blessed.

Nilkanth had specially come to Kamakshi to reform and liberate Pibek. Now that his work was over he proceeded southwards towards Balvakund and Gangasagar.

13. Ungrateful Sevakram

Nilkanth arrived at the sacred pilgrim place of Gangasagar (38 miles from Kolkata) which derives its holiness from the confluence of the river Ganga with the sea. After taking a ritual bath at the confluence, Nilkanth proceeded fearlessly through a dense forest inhabited by wild animals. Finally, he arrived at a remote village to bless Jairamdas, a pious boy.

In July 1798 Nilkanth arrived at Bhuvaneshwar. After having darshan of Bhuvaneshwar Mahadev he stayed there for three days. Nilkanth's next destination was the ancient city of Jagannath Puri. He arrived there on 26 June 1797 (A.S. 1854, Ashadh *sud* 2) and stayed by the banks of the Indradyumna lake. Here he saw thousands of fake ascetics indulging in immoral, addictive and arrogant habits. Once, an ascetic ordered Nilkanth to pluck a few spinach leaves. When he refused, the ascetic rushed at him to kill him with his *trishul*. The other ascetics came to Nilkanth's rescue, and a war broke out between the two factions. Nilkanth remained absorbed in meditation while the warring ascetics destroyed each other.

After spending six months at Jagannath Puri, Nilkanth proceeded southwards and arrived at Manaspur. Here he exposed the fake bhakti of charlatan ascetics and freed the king from their influence. Varni's next stop was Tirupati. He ascended the Venkatadri mountain and paid his respects to Bhagwan Venkateshwar. Thereafter, he took the road to Kancheepuram. On the way he came across a sannyasi called Sevakram, who was a pundit and an exponent of the Shrimad Bhagvat. He carried with him his belongings, weighing 20 kg. Sevakram was quite well off because he possessed 1000 gold coins. When Nilkanth joined him, Sevakram made him to carry his heavy load. Prior to lunch time, Sevakram would give Nilkanth a gold coin to purchase flour, ghee, gur and other food materials from the nearest village. Nilkanth would then cook food and serve Sevakram. The latter would never offer Varni anything to eat. So, Nilkanth would then go again to the same village to beg for alms and eat whatever he received. Sometimes, when he received nothing in alms he would have to fast. But still Nilkanth served Sevakram.

Once, Sevakram, out of his gluttonous nature, became ill with severe dysentery. He became extremely weak and helpless. Varni spoke to him words of comfort, "Don't worry, I will serve you." They halted at a banana grove, where Nilkanth prepared a soft bed of banana leaves for Sevakram, an arms length high, under a banyan tree. Nilkanth washed Sevakram's clothes and replaced the

banana leaves soiled by loose motions. He cooked food that suited Sevakram and also treated him with herbal medicines. After serving him Nilkanth would go to the village to beg for alms for himself and eat whatever he received.

In this way Nilkanth served him for two months till he recovered fully. Thereafter, he became robust and could digest 500 gm of ghee everyday. Subsequently, he still made Nilkanth carry his load of 20 kg. Whenever Varni would talk about God along the way, Sevakram was not interested the topic at all. After offering his sincere services, Nilkanth came to the conclusion that Sevakram was a fake and an ungrateful sannyasi. He saw that Sevakram had no love for God at all. Nilkanth thus parted from him and proceeded towards Kancheepuram.

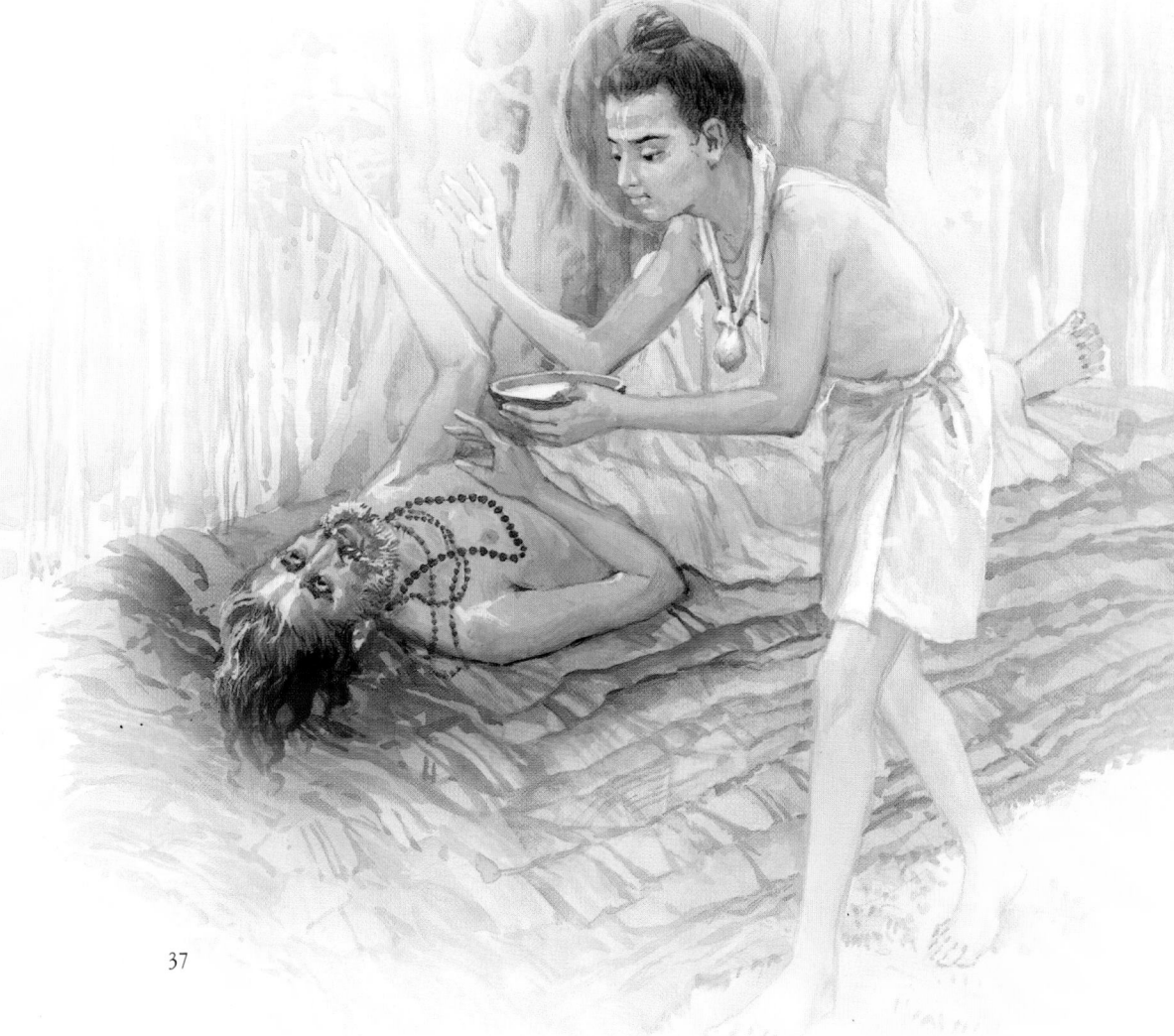

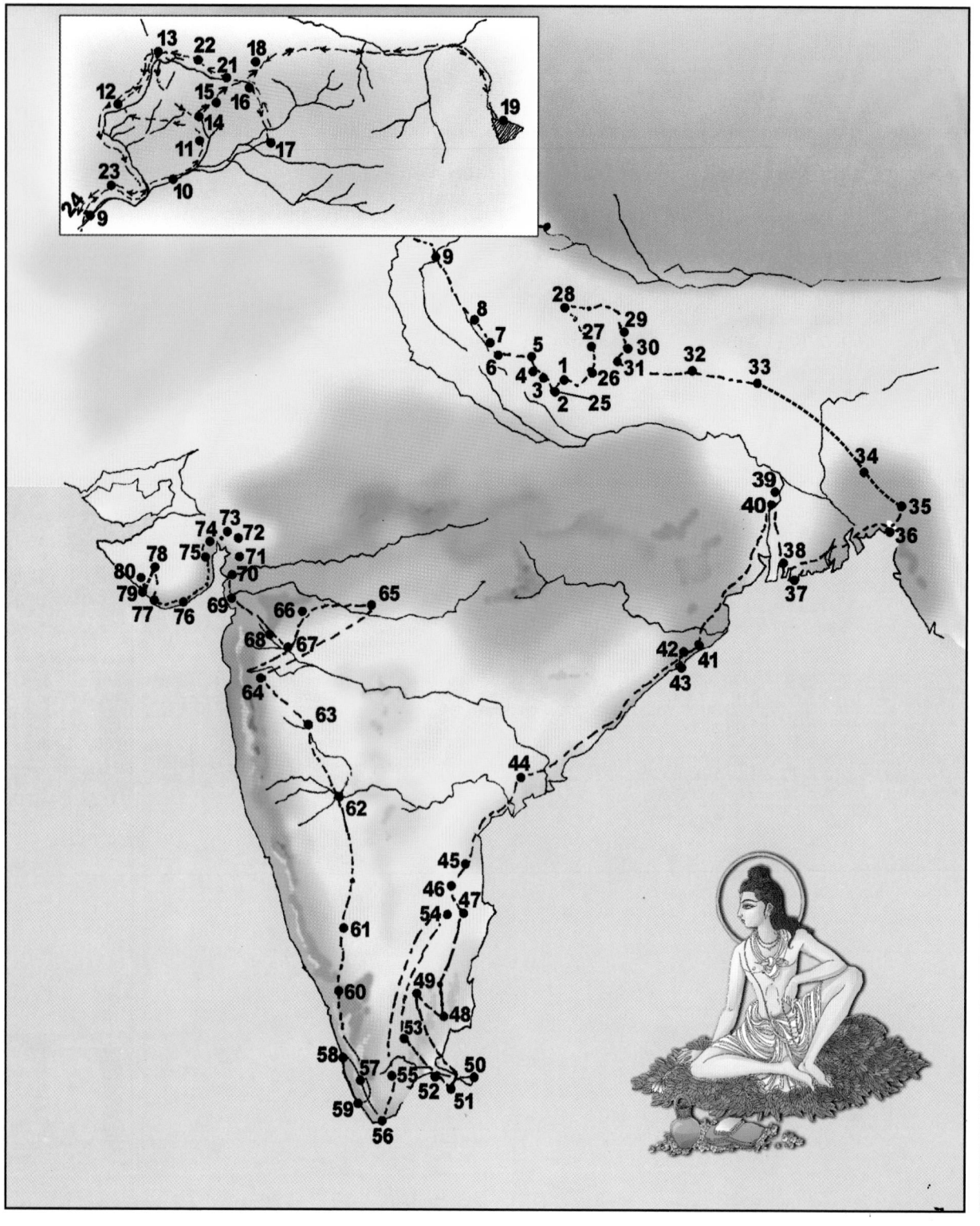

Nilkanth Varni's Pilgrimage of India

1. Chhapaiya	42. Sakshi Gopal
2. Ayodhya	43. Jagannath Puri
3. Lodheshwar	44. Adikurma
4. Jetpur	45. Pannanarsinh
5. Pathepur	46. Venkatadri
6. Naimisharanya	47. Kancheepuram
7. Sahejapur	48. Mannargudi
8. Bareli	49. Shrirang
9. Haridwar	50. Rameshwaram
10. Shripur	51. Dhanushykoti
11. Guptakashi	52. Darbhshayanam
12. Uttarkashi	53. Sundarraj
13. Guptaprayag	54. Bhutpuri
14. Gaurikund	55. Totadri
15. Kedarnath	56. Kumarikashektra
16. Badrinath	(Kanniyakumari)
17. Joshimath	57. Padmanabh
18. Mana Ghati	58. Janardan
19. Mansarovar	59. Adikeshav
20. Badrinath	60. Guruvayur
21. Badrivan	61. Melukote
22. Gangotri	62. Kishkindha
23. Lakshmanpura	63. Pandharpur
24. Haridwar	64. Pune
25. Ayodhya	65. Buranpur
26. Vanshipur	66. Malegaon
27. Kala Parvat	67. Nasik
28. Shvetgiri	68. Tryambakeshwar
29. Muktinath	69. Surat
30. Pokhra	70. Bharuch
31. Butolnagar	71. Vadodara
32. Kathmandu	72. Bochasan
33. Adivarah	73. Vartal
34. Kamakshi	74. Dholera
35. Navlakha Parvat	75. Bhavnagar
36. Balvakund	76. Guptaprayag
37. Kapilashram	77. Prabhaspatan
38. Gangasagar	78. Junagadh
39. Navdweep	79. Mangrol
40. Shantipur	80. Loj
41. Bhuvaneshwar	

Left Ayodhya: 29 June 1792 (A.S. 1849, Ashadh *sud* 10)
Arrived in Loj: 21 August 1799 (A.S. 1856, Shravan *vad* 6)
Time Taken: 7 years 1 month 11 days
Distance Travelled: Over 12,000 kms
Note: Of the 177 places that Nilkanth visited, the simplified route depicts only selected places for clarity.

14. Travels in South India

From Kancheepuram Nilkanth took the road to Shrirangkshetra, the land sanctified by Shri Ramanujacharya. On arriving there Varni bathed in the holy river Kaveri before going for darshan of the reclining four-armed *murti* of Shri Rangnathji. From here he proceeded towards Setubandh Rameshwar where Bhagwan Ram had built the bridge to Sri Lanka to vanquish Ravan and rescue Sita.

After staying for a few days in Bhutpuri Nilkanth arrived at Totadri. Here at the ashram of Jeer Swami, who was the head of the seat of the Ramanuj Sampraday, Nilkanth stayed for two months and studied the Vishishtadvait philosophy of Ramanujacharya. Then Varni proceeded to Kanyakumari, arriving in September-October 1799, during Navratri. After taking a dip in the ocean he went to Trivendrum and offered his respects to the reclining *murti* of Bhagwan Padmanabh. Then Varni proceeded to Melukote, where Ramanujacharya had stayed for 16 years. Thereafter Varni travelled to Sakshi Gopal, Kishkindha, Pampasar and Pandharpur in Maharashtra. Here, Varni visited the famous Vitthalnathji Mandir for darshan of Bhagwan Pandurang.

All along the way Nilkanth blessed and redeemed pious souls and revived the sanctity of the holy places. From Pandharpur Varni arrived at Pune and then proceeded towards Buranpur in Madhya Pradesh. From here he advanced to Malegaon where he halted at a Shiv mandir for five days. Nilkanth always found his way to the places he visited, generally without asking anyone for directions. Thereafter Nilkanth crossed the Dandakaranya (forest) and reached Nasik. After taking a dip in the holy river Godavari he had the darshan of Lord Mahadev at Tryambakeshwar. Then he entered Gujarat, the merited land that was to be his final destination in his entire pilgrimage of India. It was to become his mission field where hundreds of thousands of souls were aspiring to be redeemed by him.

Nilkanth arrived in Surat via Dharampur. From here he went to Bharuch and then visited the pilgrim spot of Shuklatirth on the banks of the river Narmada. Along the way he visited Chanod, Dabhoi and then came to the royal city of Vadodara. He met Amichand Sheth and surprised him by telling him that in future he would send his sadhus to collect the buried *murtis* of Lakshmi-Narayan in his house. Varni left and crossed the river Mahi and visited Bamangam, Umreth, Vartal and Bochasan.

He had milk and rice at Kashidas' place in Bochasan and proceeded towards Saurashtra. He arrived at Dholera, and then trudged towards Barvala and Valbhipur. Along the way, Nilkanth stayed for the night at either the Mahadev or Ramji mandirs. Thereafter, he came to Bhavnagar and then proceeded towards Gopnath and Mahuva. After arriving in the village of Shimar, Varni blessed a greedy man and proceeded to Tulsishyam and Guptaprayag. Here a pious man asked him his name. For the first time Nilkanth revealed his future name as Sahajanand. Then he proceeded to Lodhva, where he stayed for three months to accept the devotion of Lakhu Charan and bless her with moksha. Nilkanth then travelled to Mt. Girnar and blessed the sadhus engaged in austerities. Thereafter, on arriving in Piplana, Narsinh Mehta, a pious soul, was busy offering his morning puja rituals to his Shaligram. Nilkanth asked for alms at his doorstep and, with nothing ready to eat, he hurried off ahead. During that time a divine light issued from the Shaligram that Narsinh Mehta was worshipping. The experience convinced him that Nilkanth was a divine person. He requested Varni to come back and offered him alms.

Nilkanth then travelled to the village of Madhada to give darshan to Jetha Mer and his wife, who had been practising celibacy since Satyug. After blessing them, Varni proceeded to Mangrol. Govardhanbhai Sheth offered *sukhdi* as alms to Varni, who in turn redeemed his aunt, Putlibai, from the torments of hell.

After departing from Mangrol Nilkanth Varni arrived in Loj on 21 August 1799 (A.S. 1856, Shravan *vad* 6). His epic pilgrimage of India lasted for 7 years 1 month and 11 days. A new chapter was to begin with his entry into Loj.

15. Arrival in Loj

After his epic 7 years, 1 month and 11 days of pilgrimage throughout India, covering 12,000 km, Nilkanth arrived at Loj in the pre-dawn hours of Wednesday, 21 August 1799 (A.S. 1856, Shravan *vad* 6). The light showers and the lush farms on its outskirts testified to a generous monsoon. Nilkanth took his bath in the stepwell and retired into a meditative posture beneath a spreading banyan tree nearby. The women of the village routinely arrived to fill their pots with water. Their eyes suddenly fell on Nilkanth Varni. His emaciated body and the lustrous glow on his face arrested their steps. They became irresistibly drawn to the serene form of Nilkanth lost in meditation. His austerities raised several questions in their minds. They conjectured as to whether he had left his home because of the taunts from his sister-in-law or out of displeasure for his relatives. They felt how stone-hearted his mother must have been to let him take to renunciation! The women came and stood before Nilkanth, but Varni was rapt in meditation. Even their chatterings and the sound of pots clanging did not awaken or disturb Nilkanth. The women left dejectedly, reluctantly tracing their steps to the stepwell to fill their pots.

In the meantime, a sadhu from Ramanand Swami's ashram came to fill his pot from the stepwell. On seeing the gentle, teenage yogi he too was mesmerised. He came and stood before Nilkanth, waiting for him to open his eyes. He felt a surge of ineffable joy in his heart. After waiting for sometime, he too decided to fill his pot. On returning, he stood before the teenage yogi, resolving to take him to the ashram.

Shortly thereafter, Nilkanth opened his eyes. His personality glowed even more.

"Brahmachariji, where do you come from? What is your good name? Who are your parents? Why have you renounced your home? And who is your guru?" The barrage of questions mirrored the sadhu's eagerness to discover who the great Brahmachari was.

"Sadhuram! A renunciant has no caste, country and relatives. One who redeems from worldly bondage is a true parent or guru! I am in search of such a guru," Nilkanth replied softly.

The sadhu was pleased to hear Nilkanth's words. He felt that though he was young, he seemed to be spiritually enlightened. He humbly stated further, "Brahmachariji, what you say is true. But I have asked you in a social context."

Nilkanth felt the sadhu to be candid and pious. So he briefly narrated his story. Then Varni asked, "Sadhuram, what is your good name? Whose disciple are you and to what Sampraday do you belong?"

"My name is Sukhanand Swami. My guru's name is Ramanand Swami. He has an ashram here where fifty sadhus reside."

"Where is your guru, Ramanand Swami, at present?" Nilkanth enquired with a desire to meet him.

"At present he is touring in Kutch, but his principle disciple, Muktanand Swami, is here. He is very saintly and virtuous." Sukhanand Swami then paused for a while. "Please come to our ashram," he added. "Muktanand Swami and the sadhus of the ashram will be very happy to have your darshan. Our ashram will also be sanctified by your holy footprints."

Nilkanth Varni liked the sadhu's humble manners and friendly nature; but he was disinclined to go into the village. "Sadhuram, I do not go to places where there are lots of people. Wherever I have travelled I have always preferred the solitude of the forests."

Shukhanand Swami was disheartened at Nilkanth's words. He prayed again, "But my Lord, you are a great personality. Your darshan is rare even for the gods. On merely seeing you, the spiritual endeavours of the sadhus in our ashram will become fulfilled. Please grace us or else I shall call our senior sadhu, Muktanand Swami, to come and request you."

Nilkanth felt a desire to meet Muktanand Swami and the other sadhus of the ashram. He also wished to know about guru Ramanand Swami. So he got up and came to the ashram with Sukhanand Swami. Muktanand Swami was standing at the entrance. Nilkanth inferred the calm and sober sadhu to be Muktanand Swami. Varni bowed to him and Muktanand Swami welcomed him into the ashram. "Our ashram has been blessed by your presence," he said. Soon, the sadhus of the ashram gathered for Nilkanth's darshan. They, too, offered their respects to him.

Then Nilkanth revealed to Muktanand Swami, "My mind is at peace in your ashram. The sadhus here are of a peaceful disposition." "You may ask freely whatever questions you have," Muktanand Swami said.

Then Nilkanth posed the five questions he had been asking throughout his travels. Muktanand Swami satisfactorily elaborated upon the natures of *jiva, ishwar, maya,* Brahma and Parabrahma. Nilkanth was satisfied with his answers and decided to stay in the ashram for the darshan of guru Ramanand Swami. Muktanand Swami assured him that it would not be long before Ramanand Swami arrived in Loj. Nilkanth was satisfied and spent his days in the ashram.

16. Plugging the Window

It had been only a few days since Nilkanth had arrived in the ashram. One morning, according to his routine, Muktanand Swami went to discourse to a congregation of sadhus and devotees. Nilkanth, too, joined the assembly. But, on seeing women sitting packed in the assembly with the sadhus, Nilkanth got up. When Muktanand Swami told him to sit down, Varni replied, "For a sadhu to sit with women while listening to discourses, or discoursing to them, is a danger to their character. A sadhu should observe eight-fold celibacy; abstaining from seeing, touching, talking, etc. with them." Nilkanth then left the assembly. Observing *brahmacharya* is an essential discipline for the spiritual seeker who wishes to realise God. For the sadhu or ascetic the Hindu shastras prescribe eight-fold *brahmacharya*.

The following day Nilkanth told the sadhus to join him in his discourse in the mandir. Muktanand Swami then announced to the women devotees that from then onwards, at Nilkanth's order, they would no longer address them directly. Muktanand Swami also joined Nilkanth.

Though Muktanand Swami was senior to him and the foremost disciple of Ramanand Swami, Nilkanth made no compromises in establishing dharma in the ashram.

One day, Nilkanth saw a window in the ashram wall. He enquired of the sadhus as to its purpose.

"Sometimes when the embers die out fresh splinters of fire are obtained through this hole from our neighbour," replied a sadhu.

"But, who gives the splinters of fire," Nilkanth asked.

"The neighbour's wife, who else!"

Nilkanth pondered for a while. He called Muktanand Swami and advised, "Swami, this hole in the wall will one day breach the character of sadhus. It is not proper for sadhus to receive lighted splinters from women."

Then Nilkanth asked for some bricks and mortar and plugged the window himself. Muktanand Swami realised that the Hindu shastras have prescribed absolute *brahmacharya* for sadhus, and that Varni is right in disallowing any loopholes in this matter.

17. Serving the Sick

At the ashram, Nilkanth predominantly spent his entire day performing different services. After completing all his spiritual routines in the morning, he served diligently. He believed that to serve others selflessly, with the purpose of pleasing God, is bhakti.

Nilkanth, though still physically thin and weak from his travels, would bring fresh green grass from the village outskirts for the cows of the ashram each day. He would feed them and take care of them personally. He would also stroke them gently and talk to them lovingly. Such was his genuine care and love that the cows produced milk in large quantities. Varni, without the slightest hesitation, cleaned the sheds of cowdung and dirt.

Another service that he performed with compassion and sincerity was looking after the ailing sadhus. When the sadhus of the ashram saw Nilkanth serve they felt that he possessed an infinite reservoir of energy, love and patience. He made their beds, washed their clothes, placed cool cloth-pads on their heads to relieve them of fever, and served food and medicine. He often prepared special meals to suit their diet. Varni also massaged their bodies to relieve them of pain and often sat besides them to keep them company. In this way, he nursed the sick sadhus back to good health.

Everyone in the ashram was impressed by Varni's humility and sincere services.

18. Menial Services

As days passed the sadhus of the ashram in Loj came to know Varni better. Their love for him turned to respect and then to reverence. But Nilkanth was disinclined to accept adoration from others. He preferred to serve and perform the daily chores of the ashram. He would collect large leaves from the forest and make plates out of them. He gathered cowdung and wood for fuel. He would daily go to fill water from the village stepwell. He even engaged himself in the meticulous chore of cleaning grains and cooking food. No service he considered to be below his dignity. After the inmates of the ashram finished their meals, he would wash the large pots, pans and other utensils. Then during the day he would go to the surrounding villages to beg for alms. Muktanand Swami tried to restrain him from begging, but Nilkanth simply smiled and said, "I have to make efforts to complement for my lodging and boarding. Besides, without performing menial service the body will become lazy. God will be happy if I serve the sadhus."

Muktanand Swami listened silently, admiring Nilkanth's humility and spirit of service.

The great have always, through their own menial acts, revived the spirit of selfless service.

19. Teaching Meditation

Nilkanth loved to meditate. Every afternoon, Nilkanth took the sadhus to a garden opposite the ashram for meditation. He patiently taught them how to meditate. Whenever any sadhu's mind wandered off he would alert them, saying, "With your mind straying who are you meditating on?"

The sadhus realised that Nilkanth possessed the powers to read their minds. They sometimes felt whether their guru Ramanand Swami had come in the form of Nilkanth to test them and teach them.

Nilkanth was very eager for Ramanand Swami's darshan, who was away touring for *satsang* in Kutch. He had sent a message to Varni to stay in accordance to Muktanand Swami's orders.

One day Muktanand Swami told Nilkanth to don the clothes of a sadhu. Varni agreed. Then Muktanand Swami announced his new name, "Since you come from the region of river Saryu you shall be known as Sarjudas."

Nine months elapsed, and still there were no news of Ramanand Swami's arrival. Sarjudas was agitated without the guru's darshan. He knew that Muktanand Swami saw Ramanand Swami while meditating in his daily puja. So the next day Sarjudas, with his yogic powers, engaged his mind with Muktanand Swami's. The darshan of the guru brought immense joy to his heart. To everyone's amazement he described Ramanand Swami.

A month later in August 1800 Sarjudas met guru Ramanand Swami in Piplana. The master had been announcing since the arrival of Nilkanth in Loj that he was merely a drum-beater to gather the crowd and Sarjudas was the main player who had come to redeem all. He also revealed to his disciples that Sarjudas was the supreme God in human form.

On Tuesday, 28 October 1800 (A.S. 1857, Kartak *sud* 11), Ramanand Swami gave Bhagvati *diksha* to the twenty-year-old Sarjudas and named him as Sahajanand Swami and Narayan Muni.

20. Head of Fellowship

Monday, 16 November 1801 (A.S. 1858, Kartak *sud* 11) was an auspicious day in the village of Jetpur. The event was going to be a turning point in the annals of Swaminarayan history. Ramanand Swami was happy beyond description, because it was to be the fulfillment of a dream he had been nourishing and proclaiming to the Satsang community. He had given detailed instructions for the spiritual investiture to be conducted with great honour and festivity. Devotees were invited from all corners of Gujarat. Cartloads of provisions poured ceaselessly for the feast. The assembly hall and *yagna kunds* were all ready and decorated with festoons and finery befitting the occasion.

Early morning, before the pre-dawn hours, Ramanand Swami arranged a ritual bath for Sahajanand Swami by the river Bhadarganga. The entourage of sadhus and devotees went to the river bank in a grand procession of elephants, horse-drawn carriages, palanquins, and a music band. Ramanand Swami and Sahajanand Swami were seated on a decorated elephant. On reaching the river bank, the Brahmins chanted mantras and Ramanand Swami, Muktanand Swami and others performed the 16 rituals of worship of Sahajanand Swami. Thereafter, Sahajanand Swami put on a pair of new clothes, and after completing his daily puja rituals went with Ramanand Swami to the assembly hall for the spiritual coronation. The Brahmins had already started the *yagna* rituals with their sonorous mantras. The air was charged with divinity and joy. The entire hall was filled with sadhus and devotees. Sahajanand Swami and Ramanand Swami sat before the *yagna* fire and performed the rituals. Then Ramanand Swami led the twenty-one-year-old Sahajanand Swami to a decorative, high seat and officially appointed him as his successor and head of the Fellowship. The assembly hailed the name of Sahajanand Swami with thunderous applause.

Ramanand Swami then turned to the congregation and said, "O sadhus and devotees! It is a momentous day for us all. For whom I had been waiting and at whose behest I had been running this Fellowship as the guru is here before us. He is the supreme God and master of Akshardham. I have told you several times that 'I am merely the drumbeater whereas the lead player is yet to come.' And today, here before me is Sahajanand Swami who has come to establish Ekantik Dharma and to redeem and bless souls with the bliss of Akshardham." Then Ramanand Swami turned to Sahajanand Swami and said, "Today, in worldly terms, I am your guru. I have established this Sampraday. But on this day I give you the leadership of this

Sampraday. May you nourish it and inspire dharma, *gnan, vairagya* and bhakti in the hearts of all. May you redeem whoever comes in your divine association. For the purpose of *upasana* build huge mandirs and inspire the composition of shastras."

Ramanand Swami then applied the ritual *chandlo* on Sahajanand Swami's forehead. Then he personally helped Sahajanand Swami don new clothes, decorated him with jewellery and a garland of flowers.

"Swami, I am very happy with you for suppressing your spirit of renunciation to accept this seat at my word. I do not know what to give to you because you are the supreme master and the all-doer. But still I feel that I should give something as a gift to you. Pray, tell me what should I offer you."

Sahajanand Swami prostrated in veneration to guru Ramanand Swami and humbly declared, "You are my guru. Out of love and reverence you have appointed me as the head. On this occasion I would like you to bless me with two boons." The entire assembly was intrigued. Everyone was eager to know what Sahajanand Swami was going to ask.

"Swami, my heart shudders at the miseries of devotees. Therefore if your devotee is to suffer the pain of a scorpion bite then let that pain come to me multiplied millions of times in every pore of my body instead. And if your devotee is fated to have the begging bowl then let the begging bowl come to me instead, and may your devotee not be miserable because of food and clothes. I ask you to grant me these two boons. "

Ramanand Swami was simply amazed at the prayer. The entire congregation became emotional at Sahajanand Swami's profound empathy and concern for the welfare of the devotees. Ramanand Swami gestured in agreement and said, "So be it."

Then Ramanand Swami called Mulji Sharma of Bhadra on stage and introduced him to Sahajanand Swami. The latter responded, "Mulji is my abode, Akshardham. In future he will be initiated as a sadhu and be named as Gunatitanand Swami."

After the ceremonies were over a grand procession was taken out in Jetpur as a proclamation of the investiture.

With the ceremonies over, Ramanand Swami became relaxed and thought of concluding his stay on earth.

21. Samadhi to Shitaldas

Ramanand Swami travelled to the village of Faneni. He had decided to terminate his stay on earth there. The next day he caught a fever. Ramanand Swami lost all interest in food. Soon, his illness became serious and he grew extremely weak. The hour of his departure arrived. He sat in a meditative posture and made his farewell address to his disciples, "Varni is God. Believe him and obey his commands. I have gathered all of you like a drumbeater and linked you to Varni. He will establish and spread Bhagvat Dharma and bless all with final redemption." With these final words Ramanand Swami breathed his last. The day was Thursday, 17 December 1801 (A.S. 1858, Magshar *sud* 13). The entire congregation of sadhus and devotees were plunged in sadness and mourning. After the cremation rites were over, Sahajanand Swami calmed the hearts of everyone by saying, "The spiritually great never leave this earth. Think of his glory and you will experience the presence of Swami within you." His words were like a soothing balm to all.

After completing the death rites of the 12th and 13th day, Sahajanand Swami told Muktanand Swami to go to Kutch and relieve the sadness of the devotees of Ramanand Swami.

The next day, on Thursday, 31 December 1801 (A.S. 1858, Magshar *vad* 11), Sahajanand Swami announced the code of conduct for both sadhus and devotees. Then he emphasised on male-female disciplines in the Sampraday, "Where there is dharma there lies the presence of God. If you follow the moral disciplines I have prescribed then you will realise God. From now onwards I ask you to say the name of God incarnate by chanting 'Swaminarayan'."

Sahajanand Swami introduced the Swaminarayan mantra on the fourteenth day after Ramanand Swami's demise. A sannyasi called Shitaldas was seated in the assembly. Though he did not understand the discourse of Sahajanand Swami (or Shriji Maharaj) he experienced peace of mind. He got up in the middle of the assembly to touch the feet of Varni.

"Mahatma, where do you come from?" Maharaj asked.

"I come from central India and am in search of God," he replied.

"Have you found God?"

"I came to here to the west and heard that Ramanand Swami is God. But he has passed away," the sannyasi spoke in an

anguished tone.

Shri Hari then blessed him and asked, "If you have the darshan of Ramanand Swami will you stay here?" Shitaldas wondered as to how he could have the darshan of Ramanand Swami. As he was pondering Shriji Maharaj told him, "Chant the Swaminarayan mantra and Ramanand Swami will definitely give you darshan."

Shitaldas fervently desired for Ramanand Swami's darshan, so he sat cross-legged and started chanting the Swaminarayan mantra. He meditated on Maharaj and within minutes he lost consciousness and fell flat on the ground. Shriji Maharaj assured everyone that nothing serious had happened to the sannyasi; he was experiencing samadhi.

The assembly observed the gestures of Shitaldas. They saw him join hands in prayer. His face was calm and relaxed. Shitaldas saw Maharaj seated on a throne in Akshardham. Ramanand Swami and the twenty-four divine incarnations were standing praying before Maharaj. He was surprised at this divine experience. He had heard that Ramanand Swami was God but to his surprise he saw that he was praying to Bhagwan Swaminarayan.

Shitaldas offered puja to Maharaj. Then he wished to offer puja to all the liberated souls. But seeing that they were countless he wondered how it would be possible to do it. Shriji Maharaj advised him, "Why don't you wish that if Ramanand Swami is God then through his grace you may attain innumerable forms."

Shitaldas wished accordingly but nothing happened. Maharaj smiled tellingly and then advised again, "Now make a wish that out of the twenty-four incarnations if anyone is the supreme God then may you attain countless forms."

Shitaldas did likewise, but again nothing happened. Finally Maharaj said, "Now make a wish that if I am the supreme God then may you attain innumerable forms."

No sooner had Shitaldas wished, by the grace of Maharaj, he saw countless forms of himself issuing out from his body. He attained the same number of forms to that of the liberated souls. Shitaldas offered puja to all at the same time. Then on looking at Bhagwan Swaminarayan he saw infinite avatars and divine beings emanating from his form and then merging into it.

After a while Shitaldas regained consciousness. There was a divine joy on his face. He narrated to the assembly what he had seen and then added, "Maharaj is the supreme God. Ramanand Swami is his disciple."

Thereafter, Shitaldas took paramhansa *diksha* from Shri Hari and was named as Vyapakanand Swami.

22. Five Hundred Paramhansas

After the demise of Ramanand Swami, Bhagwan Swaminarayan travelled extensively for the spread of Satsang in various towns and villages. He celebrated the festivals of Janmashtmi, Jal Jhilani, Diwali, Vasant and others, gathering devotees to savour the joys of bhakti. He also introduced a new chapter in his mission through which the spiritually inclined souls experienced his divinity. Through his grace people experienced the state of samadhi, which is otherwise possible only through yoga. During samadhi people had darshan of the deities they worshipped and experienced the divinity of Bhagwan Swaminarayan.

In the village of Kalvani Muktanand Swami composed and performed *arti* of Bhagwan Swaminarayan. As the name and fame of Sahajanand Swami spread many souls were attracted and became devotees and sadhus of the Sampraday. Nityanand Swami, Nishkulanand Swami, Brahmanand Swami and many others became sadhus by virtue of the divinity they experienced in Bhagwan Swaminarayan.

With the meteoric rise of the Swaminarayan Sampraday wayward sadhus and sannyasis became infuriated. A clear distinction was becoming tangible on the social landscape as to what true saintliness is. To the wayward sadhus the virtuous, God-loving sadhus of Bhagwan Swaminarayan seemed to pose a threat to their errant habits and moral misconduct. So, they launched their bitter campaign in harassing and beating the Swaminarayan sadhus and breaking down almhouses. No sooner had they seen or come across Swaminarayan sadhus, identified by their *tilak-chandlo,* shaven head with tuft, saffron upper cloth and dhoti, *janoi* and observance of *brahmacharya* and bhakti, they would attack them mercilessly.

The sannyasis would break their *janois,* pull their tufts and cut them off, destroy the *murtis* of their personal puja and fill their eating bowls with foods that were taboo. They would purposefully bring their wives to touch them and make them fast in atonement for the breach of their vows. They would also thrash them severely. All this the Swaminarayan sadhus tolerated with silence and forgiveness. They never retaliated or wished ill of them.

After several months when the sadhus arrived in Kalvani they felt relieved of their pain and suffering at the mere darshan of Bhagwan Swaminarayan. Sahajanand Swami saw the sorry state of his sadhus. Their gaunt faces and bruised bodies reflected the extent of their sufferings. He learnt that their puja, *janoi* and *kanthi* were destroyed by the sannyasis.

Their frayed clothes, no *janois* and tufts brought tears to Maharaj's eyes. Shriji Maharaj called the senior sadhus and expressed his wish, "I want you to obey my wish by removing the *janoi, kanthi* and tuft of hair on your head. Give up your puja and perform mental worship instead. It is because of these symbols that people recognise you as Swaminarayan sadhus and persecute you. I wish you to move around as *paramhansas*."

A sadhu expressed a doubt, saying, "Maharaj, by giving up the puja and symbols of renunciation will it not thwart our spiritual sadhana?"

Shriji Maharaj assured, "Even the Pandavs, during dangerous times gave up their Kshatriya attire, weapons and symbols to stay secretly in Viratnagar at the word of Shri Krishna. Likewise, it is my wish that you accept the *paramhansa diksha*. Then the fake sadhus will not harass you in accomplishing our spiritual mission."

The words of Bhagwan Swaminarayan, who was 26 years old, were accepted by all the young and old sadhus. In only one night Sahajanand Swami initiated 500 sadhus as *paramhansas*. The landmark event was a testimony to his spiritual powers and to the absolute faith that the sadhus had vested in him as God.

Thereafter the *paramhansas* were able to travel freely without any recognition of their faith. Muktanand Swami, Gopalanand Swami, Nityanand Swami, Brahmanand Swami, Gunatitanand Swami, Premanand Swami and many others were Shriji Maharaj's *paramhansas* of the highest calibre. Their saintliness was par-excellence, and many were great scholars of Sanskrit and the Hindu shastras and highly talented in art and music. Muktanand Swami was an accomplished singer, traditional dancer, poet and an expert in Ayurved. Gopalanand Swami had mastered *ashtang*-yoga and was a great scholar in Sanskrit. Nityanand Swami was an unparalleled scholar in Sanskrit. Brahmanand Swami was an expert singer, musician, and a master of 24 different skills and arts. Premanand Swami was a matchless singer who could even change the atmosphere through his soul-stirring singing. With such an illustrious legion of *paramhansas* Bhagwan Swaminarayan ushered in a moral and spiritual renaissance on the soil of Gujarat. They travelled to towns and villages, transforming the lowest of the low from the influence of superstitions, vices and addictions.

23. Abolishes Sati Custom

Bhagwan Swaminarayan and his *paramhansas* campaigned against malpractices and evil social customs that were prevalent in 19th century Gujarat. The ignorance of people was such that they believed such immoral practices to be dharma. No amount of reasoning or explanation could stop them from their unethical ways.

The cruel custom of sati and female infanticide (*dudhpiti*) were two principal evils that were perpetrated against women in Saurashtra, Gujarat. The former practice was so barbaric that the flailing and screaming widow was forced by her in-laws to immolate herself on the funeral pyre of her husband. If she tried to escape, the in-laws would strike her and make her die with her deceased husband. Her astonishing cries for help would go unheeded because her relatives believed it to be her sacred duty to die with her husband. Such ignorance, apathy and cruelty prevailed among the people of Saurashtra. To abolish this inhuman practice Bhagwan Swaminarayan and his *paramhansas* launched a vigorous campaign against it. Bhagwan Swaminarayan explained that there was no need for a widow to follow her husband in death. She should behold God to be her spouse and spend the rest of her life in devotion and service to him. He also clarified that a widow was neither inauspicious nor an ill-omen to anyone. She, like any other human being, should be treated with sympathy and dignity.

Another social stigma practised among the Rajputs and Kathis of Saurashtra was female infanticide. Because of the dowry system the birth of a baby girl was considered to be a liability for the family. So the poor and ignorant mothers drowned their female babies in a bowl of milk, hence the name *dudhpiti*. The heartless mothers mercilessly performed this act despite the heart-rending cries of their own female babies. It was a challenge to explain to and reform mothers who were uneducated and diehard in their ways. Bhagwan Swaminarayan explained to the Rajputs that they were incurring upon themselves three unforgivable sins of killing a baby, a female and an innocent member of the family.

"But Maharaj, what can we do? We have to spend a lot of money for our daughter's marriage. It is beyond our means to spend that much. Where can we get that money? So, there is no option but to drown them in milk!" the Rajputs argued.

"But, you must stop this sin. When you need money for your daughter's marriage, I will manage to collect it from my devotees and donate it to you," Maharaj promised.

When Maharaj made this promise, the Rajputs agreed to stop their heartless and cruel practice. Thanks to Bhagwan Swaminarayan's relentless efforts the unrighteous practice was given up in Gujarat.

History bears testimony to Shriji Maharaj's effort for the uplift of women at a time when they were marginalised and persecuted. He was a champion of the women's causes, saving their lives and restoring their dignity.

24. No to Violent-Yagnas

The Vedas have propagated non-violent *yagnas* for propitiating the deities. But over time the tradition became skewed through the sacrifice of animals in the *yagna* fire. This was promulgated by Brahmin pundits to satisfy their appetite for meat-eating.

Bhagwan Swaminarayan campaigned against the malpractice of such violent *yagnas* by performing mammoth non-violent *yagnas* in the towns of Jetalpur and Dabhan. In this he preached the true purpose of *yagnas* to the thousands of Brahmins invited. He also pleased the Brahmins with vegetarian meals and by donating money as *dakshina*.

In October 1807 Shriji Maharaj was in Bhuj, Kutch. Jagjivan Mehta, the ruling authority of Bhuj, was averse to Bhagwan Swaminarayan because his followers revered him as God. During Shriji Maharaj's stay Jagjivan had arranged a *yagna* for the opening of a Shivalay he had built. He invited Bhagwan Swaminarayan to his *yagna* with the malevolent motive to insult him and challenge him in matters of scriptural knowledge and tradition. Sundarji Suthar, a devotee and the host of Shriji Maharaj, advised Maharaj not to go to the *yagna*. But Maharaj went.

Jagjivan had invited Brahmins from all parts of Gujarat to his *yagna*. He had decided to dishonour Maharaj through them. The Vammargi and Shaktipanthi Brahmins believed that animal sacrifices in *yagnas* were sanctioned by the Vedas. When Maharaj saw the animals bleating and screaming, waiting to be killed for the *yagna* he was shocked with horror. He told Kuberji, the brother of Jagjivan, "You say that the Brahmins are pious and learned, then how can they kill animals for the *yagna*. All our shastras forbid violence in *yagnas*. If they kill animals then they will lose their Brahmin qualities."

On hearing Shriji Maharaj the Brahmins realised that they could not prove that killing of animals was sanctioned by the Vedas. So they remained silent. Maharaj addressed the Brahmins, "O good people, the Yagnavalkya Smruti, Vashishta Smruti and other shastras describe the virtues of a Brahmin, namely, non-violence, performance of daily rituals in a fire, generosity, etc. The Yagnavalkya Smruti says that a Brahmin cannot attain the qualities of a Brahmin through scriptural knowledge and austerities alone. If he observes what has been ordained, then only can he be called a Brahmin. And the principal quality to be observed is that of nonviolence."

On hearing this Jagjivan flew in a rage. He shouted, "We have great Brahmin pundits here. They are conducting this *yagna* and you say it is not in accordance with the shastras. Is it only you who know the meaning of the shastras?"

Bhagwan Swaminarayan felt it was the opportune time to censure Jagjivan. He replied explicitly, "Jagjivan! The Brahmins who propagate violence in *yagnas* do not understand the Vedas. Through your coercion if animals are sacrificed in this *yagna* then the consequences will lead to your destruction."

Shriji Maharaj then left the *yagna* pandal, leaving Jagjivan in a state of intense anger.

A few days later Jagjivan Mehta met with a violent death at the hands of his superiors.

Bhagwan Swaminarayan abolished the practice of animal sacrifices in Gujarat by performing mega-*yagnas* in which grains were offered. Through them he appeased the Brahmins with generous servings of food and donations, and also enlightened them about the true practice of *yagnas* preached in the Vedas.

25. From Dust to Gold

On Sunday, 25 December 1808 (A.S. 1865, Posh *sud* 8) Shriji Maharaj inaugurated a grand *yagna* in Jetalpur. Hundreds of thousands of devotees and Brahmin pundits from all over Gujarat and also from Kashi arrived for the week long *yagna*. There were mountains of grains, gur and ghee, generously donated by devotees, to prepare meals for all the attendees.

Maharaj distributed wheat grains to all the women of Jetalpur for grinding into flour. There was joy and pride among the local womenfolk for the opportunity to offer their services. On seeing everyone proudly engaged in service, Nathi, the local prostitute, wished to serve. But then she felt unworthy for such a pious service because of her loose morals. Even the townsfolk looked upon her with disdain. She thought no one would allow her to do such meritorious service. But inspite of all the odds she resolved to approach Shriji Maharaj. She knew that he was God, and God comes to purify sinners, too.

On arriving in the assembly Nathi saw countless people listening to Maharaj. She briefly thought about how it would be possible to reach Maharaj. Then, with fortitude she started walking ahead from the women's side. To those who did not know who she was they made way for her because of her beauty and opulent clothes and ornaments. But when she came to the front the women of Jetalpur recognised her. First their voices droned in contempt, and then they created a commotion. When the menfolk realised who she was, they insulted her and stopped her from advancing any further.

Bhagwan Swaminarayan saw her amidst the commotion. He raised his hands to calm everyone down. Maharaj enquired from a local devotee as to who the lady was. "She is Nathi, the prostitute! Even her shadow corrupts anyone," the devotee replied.

"If her shadow corrupts then will not the shadow of my devotees purify her? She desires to become pure. Do you want her to remain impure?" Maharaj questioned. No one could reply to Maharaj.

"In all there lies good and bad, which purify and corrupt a person. Because you have my divine company the virtues within you are reinforced and you live a devotional life. Allow her an opportunity to reform herself." And so saying, Shriji Maharaj told the sadhus to leave the assembly. Then Maharaj beckoned the lady to come near. She came and stood before Maharaj, with her face bowed in shame.

"Sister, why have you come?" Maharaj asked.

"O Lord, because of the *yagna* going on here, there are so many women who are offering their services. Will you give me an opportunity to serve?" she requested, with the hope of cleansing herself through the service.

"We are giving wheat grains to the women to grind. Will you grind it yourself?" Maharaj asked.

"Yes, my Lord. I will grind whatever amount you give to me. I wish to be blessed in doing service for you. Though I am sinful I wish to reform my ways and become pious."

Shriji Maharaj told a devotee to give her 20 kg of wheat grains. "Go sister, grind this for the *yagna*. And do it yourself."

Nathi happily promised, "You have blessed my life today."

Everyone looked in amazement at her change in attitude and feelings.

The next day, Nathi came with the flour that she had ground herself. She placed the baskets of flour before Maharaj and offered her *pranams* to him. Then she prayed, "O Compassionate One! You have blessed me with purity. You have enabled me to experience the joy of service. My Lord, you have showered your grace upon me. Now I ask you to fulfil a favour for me."

"Was it you who took the grains to grind?" Maharaj enquired.

"Yes, Maharaj. I stayed awake all night to grind the grains. You are all-knowing, therefore you know. But still, see these hands of mine." And she showed her palms to Maharaj. Her soft hands were bruised and dotted with boils. Everyone was amazed at her sincere effort in grinding the grains.

Maharaj was pleased at her service and blessed her, "Sister, you are forgiven for all your sins. From henceforth live in purity to redeem your life."

"Maharaj, I wish you to sanctify my house that was once a den of sin. Please fulfil this dear wish of mine."

The next day Maharaj sanctified her house with Muktanand Swami, Brahmanand Swami and other *paramhansas*.

Out of his generous compassion and divine grace Bhagwan Swaminarayan reformed a sinful woman into a pure devotee, ultimately blessing her with final redemption.

Even today, the story of Nathi's transformation from dust to gold is sung in the assembly halls of the Swaminarayan mandirs as a testimony to the divine grace of Bhagwan Swaminarayan.

26. Sagram Vaghri's Hut

Sagram Vaghri lived an unethical life. His caste and habits were repugnant to the locals of the village of Limli. Born into the lowest of the low castes, he was labeled as an untouchable by the prevailing system of society 200 years ago. But his life changed radically through the association of Bhagwan Swaminarayan's *satsang*. He gave up all his vices and malpractices and became a practicing devotee. Daily puja, vegetarian diet, drinking filtered water and not coveting another's possessions were the principles of *satsang* that he and his wife imbibed in their lives.

Once, Sagram requested Shriji Maharaj to sanctify his mud-straw hut. And soon that great day arrived. In the middle of one night, Maharaj left alone on Manki, his mare, from Dada Khachar's *darbar,* in Gadhada. He had informed no one of his destination. Maharaj took the road leading to the obscure village of Limli where Sagram Vaghri resided. He reached the outskirts of Limli in the pre-dawn hours. Maharaj pulled the reins of Manki towards Sagram's hut. Then he called out, "Sagram, Sagram!"

Sagram recognised Maharaj's voice. He hurriedly opened his door and welcome Maharaj. Both he and his wife were elated at the sudden arrival of their Lord. They quickly laid out a bed for Maharaj to sit on. Then Sagram's wife went to fetch fresh water for Maharaj. Sagram engaged himself in Shriji Maharaj's darshan. He could not believe that his Lord had come to his ordinary hut. For him it was the fulfilment of a cherished wish. In a surge of joy he danced and sang ecstatically, "An elephant has entered into my hut!"

Shriji Maharaj was pleased at Sagram's love and devotion. Maharaj told Sagram that he was hungry. "It won't take long to prepare *rotla* and cook aubergines," Sagram replied. Within no time the food was ready. Maharaj ate the simple meal in the early hours of the morning. It was Sagram's hospitality and love that Maharaj was savouring.

Maharaj's mission to fulfil Sagram's wish was accomplished. He departed from Limli later in the day.

Bhagwan Swaminarayan redeemed all regardless of caste, creed or colour. He served and moralised the downtrodden classes and reformed them into sterling devotees and law abiding citizens.

Once, Sagram and his wife were on their way to Surat to eke out a living because of the severe drought that had hit their region. On the way they found a silver anklet. Sagram was tempted to take it, but on remembering Maharaj's injunction, not to covet another's possessions, he refrained. He covered it up with dust. When his wife enquired what he had done, Sagram told her that he had covered the anklet with dust so that she would not be enticed into taking it. But Sagram's wife replied, "You merely covered dust with dust. I believe another's possessions to be nothing but dust."

Bhagwan Swaminarayan instilled such high morals and spirituality in even the lowest and downtrodden members of the society. Sagram Vaghri is forever remembered in the Swaminarayan Sampraday for his integrity, devotion and purity.

27. Joban Pagi

On 2 January 1810, hundreds of thousands of Brahmins and devotees had arrived for the 18-day grand *yagna* in Dabhan. Bhagwan Swaminarayan performed non-violent *yagnas* to reestablish the pristine Vedic *yagna* tradition and counteract the practice of violent *yagnas* in which animals were sacrificed.

The Hindu shastras explain that the *yagna* tradition is a means to appease and offer gratitude to the deities who contribute in sustaining all life forms.

During this *yagna*, a notorious dacoit named Joban Pagi of Vartal came to know about the thorough bred stallion, Rozo, that belonged to Bhagwan Swaminarayan. Joban and his eighteen companions decided to steal Rozo and other excellent horses that belonged to the Kathi devotees. They came late at night when the entire camp of devotees was in deep sleep. Despite the vigilant security patrols Joban and his men entered the stables after midnight. Joban was armed with a sword and dagger. Half his face and head was covered with a muffler. When he advanced towards Rozo, he suddenly stopped midway because of what he saw. The illustrious figure of Bhagwan Swaminarayan was standing by each of the horses. He was either patting them, feeding them or making them drink water. Joban could not believe his eyes. He wondered as to how Swaminarayan could have so many forms. Since there was no chance to take the horses away. Joban and his men retreated, putting off their mission for the following night.

The next night, Joban again arrived to steal Rozo. But once again he saw Bhagwan Swaminarayan attending to every horse. Joban was simply stunned by the experience. He felt that Swaminarayan must be a master magician to assume so many forms at once. He returned crestfallen. Joban told his companions that they had one more night to try before the *yagna* concluded the day after. But when they came the next night, they faced the same situation of Maharaj tending to the horses.

The next morning, Joban and his men came and sat at the back of the assembly. On seeing Shriji Maharaj they realised he was the same person they had seen in the stables for three nights. When Maharaj saw them, he called them to the front. "Provide them with provisions of ghee, sugar and flour. For three days they have been hungry and spending sleepless nights. They are now very tired and hungry," Maharaj instructed an attendant. On hearing this Joban Pagi and his companions placed their weapons at

the feet of Maharaj and prayed, "Maharaj, we have committed a crime in a holy place where our sins can be washed away."

The entire assembly was stunned on learning of Joban Pagi's presence. They felt how could he and his men have come here in spite of the heavy security!

Joban shed tears of repentance and said, "Maharaj, for three nights we made attempts to steal your Rozo horse and the excellent breed of horses belonging to the Kathi Darbars. But in all the stables we entered, we saw your divine form before each and every horse during all the three nights. Then we thought you must be God."

Seeing the repentant Joban, Maharaj called him nearer and placed his hands in a gesture of benediction on his head. "Joban, it pleases me that you have come to take refuge," Maharaj began. "But if you give up your immoral ways and base nature then only will I accept you. By wearing the *kanthi* today if you return to your wayward ways tomorrow, then dharma will not protect you."

As Joban was listening to Shriji Maharaj's words he experienced a flashback of all his sinful acts in his mind.

A shudder of fear ran down his spine. He fell at Maharaj's feet and entreated, "O God, I shall do as you command. I pledge to give up all my sinful ways. I bow at your feet. My time to be saved has arrived. Maharaj, protect this wretch and sinner by accepting me. "

Bhagwan Swaminarayan felt that Joban was speaking from his heart. They were words of regret and repentance. Maharaj initiated him and his companions into Satsang. "Now listen Joban. From today you have to abstain from drinking liquor, eating meat, stealing and adultery."

Joban felt blessed and promised, "Maharaj, I will obey these commands no matter what happens. I shall chant your holy name and remember your divine form in my heart."

Bhagwan Swaminarayan was pleased with Joban Pagi's change of heart. The entire congregation was dumbfounded at the transformation of Joban Pagi. They knew about his reign of terror. Such was his power and notoriety that hard-core criminals and thieves on the way to Kolkata would not dare touch a traveller carrying his arrow.

During his entire ministry Bhagwan Swaminarayan reformed many sinners into law abiding citizens and devotees. The miracle of transforming lives is the greatest of all miracles.

28. Diksha of Mulji Sharma

In 1807, Bhagwan Swaminarayan had visited the nondescript village of Bhadra. For the first time he revealed the glory of Mulji Sharma to his mother, Sakarba. "Mulji is my eternal abode and choicest disciple," Maharaj stated. "He is Aksharbrahma. There are countless universes floating in every pore of his body. He is all-pervading and eternally in communion with me. Only through realising his glory and identifying one's *atma* with him does one realise my greatness and attain me."

A few years later, on 2 January 1810, Shriji Maharaj arranged a grand *yagna* for the *diksha* of Mulji Sharma at Dabhan. Brahmin pundits and devotees arrived in multitudes from all parts of Gujarat and India. The *yagna* began in the presence of Maharaj with the chanting of Vedic mantras by Brahmins. The Vammargi Brahmins, who were preparing meals in the kitchen, tried to create a furore by emptying the ghee vessels and dumping the laddus in the village pond. But Bhagwan Swaminarayan replenished the empty ghee vessels through his divine powers.

The glory of the grand *yagna* spread to all parts of Gujarat. More and more Brahmins flocked in large numbers and recognised the essence of nonviolence as the prerequisite in the Vedic *yagna* tradition.

On the eve of the concluding day, Bhagwan Swaminarayan informed a devotee looking after the *yagna* arrangements, "Tomorrow I wish to give Bhagvati *diksha* to Mulji Sharma of Bhadra. I have arranged this grand *yagna* specially for his *diksha*. In future you will all realise his divine glory."

The next day on 20 January 1810 (A.S. 1866, Posh *sud* 15) the *yagna* pandal resonated with the mellifluous chanting of Vedic mantras by Brahmins. The *yagna* pit was blazing with the offerings of ghee and grains. The devotees and sadhus were eagerly awaiting the arrival of Mulji Sharma. When Mulji arrived he was donned in a saffron dhoti, *janoi* and had his head shaven. Shriji Maharaj himself performed the *diksha* rituals. Everyone was intrigued as to who Mulji was, because never before had Maharaj given *diksha* to anyone by arranging a *yagna* and inviting a mammoth gathering.

Shriji Maharaj, perceiving the inner thoughts of the congregation, raised his two hands and addressed the assembly, "O sadhus and devotees, today I am initiating Mulji Sharma on this auspicious occasion. He is a Brahmin from the village of Bhadra. Though he looks ordinary, he is my abode, Akshardham, beholding me and countless *muktas*. In his manifest form he forever serves me. Just as you see him here he is similarly serving me in Akshardham. He has infinite redemptory virtues, he is the all-doer and also the non-doer, he is above the three *gunas* and is therefore *gunatit,* and he has the fullest knowledge of my form. Through him my glory shall spread." Thereafter the *diksha* rituals continued.

In conclusion, Maharaj declared his name, "Since Mulji is above the three *gunas,* I name him 'Gunatitanand'. His glory shall spread throughout the world."

Later, Gunatitanand Swami became renowned as the ideal devotee and the first spiritual successor of Bhagwan Swaminarayan. He spread the supreme glory of Shriji Maharaj as God in the Swaminarayan Sampraday. He is worshipped as the choicest devotee and as Aksharbrahma, in consonance with the Bhakta-Bhagwan Vedic tradition, in the Bochasanwasi Shri Akshar Purushottam Swaminarayan Sanstha (BAPS).

The *diksha* of Gunatitanand Swami was a landmark event in the annals of the Swaminarayan Sampraday, because he later continued the mission of Bhagwan Swaminarayan in establishing Bhagvat Dharma – inspiring dharma, *gnan*, *vairagya* and bhakti – and guiding all spiritual seekers onto the path of final liberation.

29. All Compassionate

The monsoon of 1811 had not arrived. The people of Saurashtra were short of water. The land had turned barren and parched. The heat was unbearable. Under these circumstances Jiva Khachar and Rathod Dhadhal requested Shriji Maharaj to bless the soil of Sarangpur with his holy feet. "Your arrival will bless our land with rains," they said. Maharaj agreed, and arrived in Sarangpur the next day with a few of his sadhus and devotees. While Maharaj was having dinner, Jiva Khachar described the extent of the drought in his region. "Maharaj, there is not a drop of water around. The cattle are dying because they have nothing to drink."

"Indra, the rain god, is sulking, but he will have to rain for devotees like you," Maharaj blessed. Then Shriji Maharaj briefly glanced in the north-easterly direction. The setting sun was retiring for the day. It had mercilessly scorched the earth for another day. Then suddenly a black cloud appeared from nowhere in the skies. Maharaj started chanting the name of God. With the growing intensity of the chanting, the cloud increased in size. In a short while lightning streaked across the skies. The deafening crack of thunder resonated on earth and in sky.

"Maharaj, it seems that Indra is arriving," Jiva Khachar enquired.

"Yes, he is approaching angrily. He will rain in torrents. At present we are at a loss for water, but after its arrival there will be a greater loss because of water," Maharaj spoke prophetically. But no one understood Maharaj's words.

The rains came. The land became wet and exuded a typical monsoon aroma. Slowly the rains increased in intensity. The frequency of lightning and thunder heightened. Soon it rained like cats and dogs. The mud houses in the village started collapsing. Jiva Khachar informed Maharaj of the situation and prayed to him to stop the rains.

"Now Indra is in tantrums. Your house, too, will collapse soon and there will be no way to get outside. Quickly, take me to another house."

Jiva Khachar took Shriji Maharaj to his new house. From there he surveyed the damage caused by Indra's wrath. Jiva Khachar left to see the state of his village and returned to inform Maharaj about the extent of destruction. Then late at night, for fear of the new house collapsing, Maharaj was transferred to the nearby house of another devotee. Jiva Khachar left to help

those who had lost their homes. He helped his people and transferred their cattle towards shelter and safety. On returning, Maharaj said, "Bapu! You have done what befits a chief. The village chief should solve the miseries of his citizens first."

In the middle of the night, Maharaj was awakened by a loud plea, "O God! Come quickly. The main beam of my house is ready to collapse at any moment. It will crush my children and cattle to death."

Shriji Maharaj quickly slipped outside alone, not even wakening up his attendant, Mulji Brahmachari. He ran in the direction of the plea and reached the house. Maharaj saw that the main beam was broken and on the verge of coming down. Immediately, Maharaj bore the burden of the broken beam on one of his shoulders. Both Lakha and Deva Patel, the residents, were surprised with what they saw. They thought it would require ten to fifteen people to bear the beam, and the visitor was supporting it single-handedly. In the darkness they couldn't recognise who it was. Maharaj hurriedly ordered, "Take your family and cattle urgently to safety outside. Your entire house is standing only on this beam which is resting on my shoulder. It will break at any moment."

Both Deva and Lakha untethered their cattle and led them and their family outside the house to safety. Then Shriji Maharaj placed the broken beam on the ground and disappeared into the night. No sooner had Maharaj left, the roof came crashing down.

Bhagwan Swaminarayan returned to the house of Jiva Khachar and went to sleep. Soon thereafter, the rains subsided.

The next morning, while Mulji Brahmachari was bathing Maharaj he saw a deep cut on his shoulder. "Maharaj, how did you get this deep cut on you shoulder?" the Brahmachari asked.

When Maharaj described what had happened, the Brahmachari was annoyed and retorted, "Couldn't you have woken me up!"

"You were in deep sleep! If I had waited to wake you up, then all his cattle and family members would have died."

"But Deva Patel is not a devotee!" exclaimed Mulji Brahmachari.

"That is true, but he called out to God for help. So, I had to go!"

Mulji understood that God always protects those who seek his help. By that time Jiva Khachar arrived and informed Maharaj about the fate of Deva Patel's house. "Maharaj, it was so brave and compassionate of someone to have rushed to help

him. That person shouldered the main beam and saved his family members and cattle from being crushed to death."

Shriji Maharaj simply smiled as he listened to Jiva Khachar's account. Then Mulji Brahmachari revealed, "Bapu! That person who shouldered the massive beam was Maharaj himself. Look at this deep gash on his shoulder."

Jiva Khachar was deeply touched by Maharaj's empathy and service to an ordinary villager like Deva Patel. He realised that God serves all, regardless of class or status. This act of Maharaj is forever celebrated in the Sampraday as an ideal of service to humanity in times of calamity or catastrophe.

30. "Sadguru Khele Vasant..."

In 1812 Shriji Maharaj exuberantly celebrated the festival of colours, Fuldol, in the small village of Sarangpur. Everyone, including Maharaj, sadhus and the devotees, sprinkled and sprayed colours upon each other. The air was awash with kumkum and scented coloured water. The exotic ambience of devotion, festivity and tradition infused a fresh lease of joy in the hearts of devotees. It provided a welcome break from the monotony and lethargy of daily rural life.

That same evening everyone gathered in the precincts of Rathod Dhadhal's home. When Bhagwan Swaminarayan arrived, all the sadhus arranged themselves in pairs to form a circle in order to play *ras* with Maharaj. Gunatitanand Swami stood opposite Maharaj as his partner. Shriji Maharaj proclaimed, "Oh, he is a Sadguru!"

Everyone was surprised to hear this because it had been only two years since Gunatitanand Swami had been initiated as a sadhu. How could he be a *sadguru* so soon!

Shriji Maharaj then started playing *ras* while singing the devotional verses of Kabir:

Jogiyā tālat janam kerā fānsalā....

Premnā pyālā Jogiyā, Jug Jug Jivo so Jogiyā...

Koti Krishna jode hāth, koti Vishnu name māth,

Koti Shankar dhare dhyān, koti Brahmā kathe gnān,

Sadguru khele Vasant...

"The noose of the cycle of births is removed by the realised Sadhu. They are the cup of love. May they live for all time.

Before him stand millions of Krishnas with folded hands and millions of Vishnus with bowed heads.

Millions of Shivs meditate on him and millions of Brahmas speak of his glory.

The Sadguru is engaged in the divine play of the spring."

As Maharaj sang each verse the sadhus chorused after him. The thunderous sound of drums and the sweet notes of the shehnais transformed the grounds of Rathod Dhadhal into a festive atmosphere.

Maharaj touched his stick often on the chest of Gunatitanand Swami as he sang Kabir's verses. The pace of *ras* increased.

In the presence of Maharaj time and fatigue disappeared. Everyone was absorbed in devotion, striking their *ras* sticks with enthusiasm. Then suddenly, Maharaj stopped and the *ras* came to a halt. Shriji Maharaj called Muktanand Swami and Anandanand Swami and asked, "Who is the Sadguru described in this verse?"

"Maharaj, it is you," they replied.

"I am the supreme God, and the Sadguru whose glory is sung in this verse is Gunatitanand Swami," Maharaj proclaimed.

But no one understood the words of Maharaj. It was difficult to believe that Gunatitanand Swami was the Sadguru, because of his young age and simple ways.

Shriji Maharaj repeated what he had said, "O Sadhus, listen. These verses were composed by Kabirji; who believed God to have a human form. He knew that Aksharbrahma is my abode, Akshardham, and that he eternally serves me and the *muktas* as our abode. And that Akshar is this Gunatitanand Swami! He is the eternal Sadguru and the gateway to moksha. When you realise him, then you will know me fully."

On many occasions Bhagwan Swaminarayan revealed Gunatitanand Swami as his eternal abode, Akshardham, and as his ideal devotee, Akshar or Aksharbrahma. This is in consonance with the Vedic tradition of Bhakta and Bhagwan, where Shriji Maharaj is Bhagwan and Gunatitanand Swami is his ideal Bhakta in the Swaminarayan Sampraday.

31. Singers from Gwalior

Bhagwan Swaminarayan had an illustrious legion of *paramhansas*. They were not only adept in spirituality, but also masters of various skills and arts. Among his eight saint-poets, Premanand Swami was the most accomplished singer. His soulful singing and mastery in traditional classical music impressed even the king of Junagadh. Once when some renowned Muslim singers from Gwalior came to perform before the Nawab of Junagadh, he said, "Go and listen first to the soulful singing of the Swaminarayan sadhu, Premanand Swami. After that if you feel you can sing better than him, then come back and I shall listen to you."

The singers of Gwalior travelled to Gadhada. It was evening time when they arrived at Dada Khachar's *darbar*. Shriji Maharaj was discoursing in the *darbar,* beneath the neem tree. The singers offered their respects to Maharaj. Then they explained the purpose of their visit. Maharaj told Premanand Swami to sing *rag* Bhairav. Without the slightest hesitation, Premanand Swami prepared himself to sing *rag* Bhairav. The guest singers were amused at Maharaj's command which was totally opposite to the norms of classical music. They felt that the *rag* meant to be sung during early morning should not be presented in the evening. But when Premanand Swami started singing the *alap,* followed by his mellifluous rendering of *"Chandan charchit nil kalevar sundar..."* there was a radical change in the surrounding ambience. To everyone's surprise evening put on a morning attire. The sight of birds chirping and fluttering their wings as they flew from their nests was similar to the post-dawn orchestra of nature. A cool breeze wafted through the assembly. The transformation of the hot evening into a cool morning became more pronounced as Premanand Swami sang with his heart.

The maestros from Gwalior were stunned at Premanand Swami's profound singing. They realised the glory of Bhagwan Swaminarayan and offered their obeisances to him before leaving for Gwalior.

The other celebrated saint-poets of Bhagwan Swaminarayan were Muktanand Swami, Brahmanand Swami, Devanand Swami, Nishkulanand Swami, Manjukeshanand Swami, Bhumanand Swami and Dayanand Swami. In all, they have composed more than 16,000 bhajans describing the form and glory of Shriji Maharaj.

32. Queen Kushalkunvarba

Two hundred years ago Dharampur was a royal state in south Gujarat. The ruling monarch was the prudent and pious Queen Kushalkunvarba. She was conducting the affairs of the state on behalf of her grandson, Vijaydev, who was still underage to assume the royal responsibilities. One day, she came to hear about the glory of Bhagwan Swaminarayan through the discourses of one of his *paramhansas*, Paramchaitanyanand Swami. As a result, she developed a fervent desire to have Maharaj's darshan and to invite him and to receive his blessings. She sent an invitation to Gadhada. Sensing her genuine love and devotion, Maharaj embarked upon the 400 km journey from Gadhada to Dharampur. He took a large entourage of *paramhansas* and devotees with him. The Rajput devotees were ever vigilant to ward off dacoits and wild animals along the way.

On the outskirts of Dharampur, Kushalkunvarba had arranged a grand, royal welcome for Maharaj. The crown prince, Vijaydev, and the principal minister of state were waiting to receive him. When they saw Maharaj, both the prince and the minister galloped towards him and offered prostrations. Shriji Maharaj was requested to sit on a decorated elephant and Vijaydev fanned him with a flywhisk. The procession commenced with a gun salute and music provided by the royal infantry and band. The senior *paramhansas* were accommodated in chariots and palanquins. The entire city of Dharampur was decorated with bunting, festoons of leaves and fragrant flowers, and giant archways. People sprayed perfume from the galleries of their homes as Maharaj passed by. Many showered flowers and rice grains to honour and welcome the entire entourage. The procession finally arrived at the royal palace. When Maharaj alighted from the elephant, Queen Kushalkunvarba welcomed him with a garland and offered her prostrations. Then she stood looking at Maharaj, imprinting his divine form in her heart. Tears of joy welled up, "O Lord, you have arrived. You made me pine for your darshan for a long time. Now my desire has been fulfilled."

Prince Vijaydev performed the puja of Maharaj and welcomed him inside the royal palace. The *paramhansas* and devotees were accomodated in adjacent buildings.

Day after day, Maharaj enlightened the queen and the people of Dharampur with his discourses and the singing of bhajans by his *paramhansas*. Kushalkunvarba made sure there were no lapses in their services to all the guests.

Once at midnight, Maharaj informed Mulji Brahmachari that he was hungry. Kushalkunvarba personally baked *rotla* in the middle of night, and served it with curds and pickles.

Shriji Maharaj celebrated the festival of colours (Rangotsav) in Dharampur and delighted the devotees by sprinkling kumkum and spraying coloured water. That same evening Maharaj told the Queen that he would be leaving the next day. Kushalkunvarba pondered as to what would happen to her after Maharaj's departure. Then, she asked, "Maharaj, you had written in your first letter that you were writing from Anirdesh. Kindly explain where is Anirdesh."

Maharaj revealed, "This palace of yours is pointable *(nirdesh)*, but the earth in comparison is unpointable *(anirdesh)*. Then our earth is pointable, but water is not. Water is pointable, but light is unpointable…" Maharaj continued describing the cosmic elements and abodes in this manner. Finally, he said, "My abode, Akshardham, is *anirdesh*, because it is above maya and infinite in size."

While Shriji Maharaj was explaining this, Kushalkunvarba etched the *murti* of Maharaj in her heart.

Then in the evening Kushalkunvarba arranged an assembly in her palace. It was to be the last evening of Maharaj's stay there. She wished that Shriji Maharaj bless everyone for the last time. Maharaj sat on the royal throne. She sat before him with her grandson, prince Vijaydev. The prince worshipped Maharaj's holy feet. He then performed *pujan* of Maharaj, offered him royal clothes and a garland of flowers. Then the palace officials performed the *pujan* of Maharaj and offered gifts to him. Thereafter, prince Vijaydev performed the *pujan* of the sadhus, who were standing some distance away from Maharaj.

"Maharaj, why don't you accept this kingdom?" Kushalkunvarba requested. "Ever since I realised your glory through your *paramhansas*, I have been ruling this kingdom with the feeling that this is all yours. Now that the owner is here, it is my wish to give your kingdom back to you."

Shriji Maharaj smiled and replied, "O Queen Mother, you have as yet not realised my true glory. By my wish countless universes are created and destroyed. Of what measure is your kingdom of 500 villages! I have not come to rule kingdoms. I have come to destroy evil and establish Bhagvat Dharma. I still have work to be done. Therefore, you rule your kingdom; and do not become attached to it. Other than myself if you nourish a desire for anything mundane, then you'll have to take another birth."

Kushalkunvarba assured Maharaj that there was nothing in her heart other than his divine form. Maharaj blessed the queen with a print of his footprints on a silk cloth. The next day, Shriji Maharaj was given a royal farewell.

Fifteen days later Kushalkunvarba passed away, forever earning a place among the divine *muktas* in Akshardham.

Bhagwan Swaminarayan, through his divine charisma, inspired sterling devotion and faith in women devotees like Kushalkunvarba, Laduba, Jivuba, Rajbai and many others. Through the ages the Swaminarayan Sampraday has nourished faith, integrity and devotion in women and made them the recipients of the highest grace of God.

33. Festival of Colours

Bhagwan Swaminarayan celebrated the spectrum of Hindu festivals in their pristine tradition to revive and consolidate faith, bhakti, morality and a spirit of camaraderie in society. He celebrated Shivratri, Holi, Fuldol, Ram Navmi, Janmashtmi, Jal Jhilani, Diwali, Annakut and other festivals, to make the pious and the impious eligible for redemption. He put special emphasis on the observance of morality and discipline between men and women during festivals to preserve the flavour of pure bhakti and joy.

Bhagwan Swaminarayan celebrated the annual Rangotsav or festival of colours, following the celebration of Holi, with pomp and devotion. Once, in Vartal, Maharaj gave orders for the celebration of the festival of colours. The venue was the lush mango grove in Gnanbaug, Vartal. Devotees from all over Gujarat started flocking in thousands. The precincts of Vartal were overflowing with a concourse of *paramhansas* and devotees. Nishkulanand Swami had made a twelve door *hindolo*. Maharaj gave darshan in the *hindolo* while the sadhus sang the *hindolo* bhajans.

After lunch Maharaj returned to Gnanbaug to celebrate the Rangotsav. The pots and reservoirs were filled with kumkum and naturally coloured water. Shriji Maharaj sanctified the water troughs with his feet. Thereafter the festival commenced. Sprays of coloured water issued from squirters in all directions. Soon the frenzy of devotion saturated the air and earth in a pastel of colours and joy. Bhagwan Swaminarayan squirted coloured water alternately on the *paramhansas* and the devotees. The rhythm of drums and the sound of shehnais increased the tempo of the divine sport. Maharaj entertained everyone with the divine bliss of Akshardham. The joy of colouring others and the blessing of being coloured by Shriji Maharaj was imprinted in the minds of all.

The festival concluded with a clap from Shriji Maharaj. The entire gathering then bathed in the local pond to clean themselves.

Shriji Maharaj revealed that he celebrated festivals because even the slightest memory of it during the time of death would redeem the devotee or sinner. Such was the glory he attributed to spiritual festivals.

34. The Vachanamrut

Bhagwan Swaminarayan enlightened and motivated his congregations through his spiritual discourses. He beautifully communicated the esoteric truths of the Hindu shastras in the most down-to-earth manner. His dialogue style of presentation riveted the *paramhansas* and rural devotees in his assemblies. He encouraged them to think, understand and practise spirituality in their daily lives. He candidly reveals, "What I am about to say to you, I say not out of pretence, or out of self-conceit, or to spread my own greatness." Such personal purity and transparency proves the worth of his discourses that are compiled into a shastra called the Vachanamrut – the nectarine words.

From 1819 to 1829 his discourses were scribed by four of his scholarly *paramhansas*, namely, Muktanand Swami, Gopalanand Swami, Nityanand Swami and Shukanand Swami. They edited and compiled them into 273 discourses, encapsulating the timeless wisdom of the Vedas, Upanishads, Brahmasutras, Bhagvat Gita, Shrimad Bhagvad, etc. The Vachanamrut is the most sacred shastra in the Swaminarayan Sampraday, read daily by its followers.

The first paragraph of each discourse in the Vachanamrut vividly chronicles the time, day, date, year, name of place and the clothes and decorations worn by Maharaj. The Vachanamruts were delivered in the villages of Gadhada, Sarangpur, Kariyani, Loya, Panchala, Vartal, Amdavad, Aslali and Jetalpur.

In Gadhada, where Bhagwan Swaminarayan predominantly stayed, Maharaj discoursed beneath a neem tree in the *darbar* of Dada Khachar. He invariably wore white clothes and, akin to the Upanishadic dialogue tradition, he commenced his discourse by either asking a question or inspiring the audience to voice their questions. The serene ambience of Gadhada provided a perfect backdrop to his profound spiritual dialogues. The content of the Vachanamrut is basically spiritual and philosophical, dealing with the nature of *jiva, ishwar, maya*, Brahma and Parabrahma. It also includes the concept of moksha, the indispensability of guru, happiness, misery, non-violence, prayer, bhakti, morals, good company, service, positive attitude, introspection, dhyan and many practical aspects of daily life and spiritual sadhana. The Vachanamrut is a goldmine of knowledge, inspiration and divinity for all spiritual seekers. The divine words of Bhagwan Swaminarayan provide practical answers and solutions to all types of spiritual enquiries and problems.

35. The Shikshapatri

In the final years of his life, Bhagwan Swaminarayan decided to write a code of conduct for all his disciples: *brahmacharis,* sadhus, householders, kings, married women and widows. He wished to include the essence of the Shruti and Smruti shastras in a succinct book.

Maharaj commenced writing the Shikshapatri, a booklet of moral instructions, in the Hindu New Year of 1882 (1826 CE) in Vartal. He wrote 212 verses in Sanskrit, completing it on 25 January 1826 (A.S. 1882, Vasant Panchmi). This historic day is remembered and celebrated in the Swaminarayan Sampraday as the birthday of the Shikshapatri. The sadhus and devotees perform *pujan* of the Shikshapatri out of reverence and honour. This landmark contribution of Bhagwan Swaminarayan provided the Sampraday and all its devotees with a moral and spiritual constitution to abide by. It instructs on matters regarding health, hygiene, dress code, diet, etiquette, diplomacy for the royalty, finance, trade, education, friendship, morality, austerity, atonement, celebrations, religious duties, Bhakta-Bhagwan mode of worship and the aim of life.

The moral codes are applicable to people of all classes and stages of life – young and old; men and women; married, unmarried and widowed; and householders and sadhus. Bhagwan Swaminarayan writes that whosoever obeys the Shikshapatri shall be happy in this world and the world hereafter. He adds that it is for the good of all people.

The Shikshapatri is a manual for mankind that inspires both outer and inner purity in individuals. The three fundamental purities that he emphasises about are: (1) Purity of Diet, (2) Purity of Conduct, and (3) Purity of Soul.

(1) **Purity of Diet:** He forbids his disciples from eating meat, eggs, onions and garlic. Alcohol, tobacco and drugs are also a taboo.

(2) **Purity of Conduct:** He ordains not to be disrespectful to any deities, pilgrim places, chaste women, sadhus and the Vedas. He forbids adultery, gambling and bad company. For sadhus he has prescribed absolute *brahmacharya.*

(3) **Purity of Soul:** The final liberation of a soul is attained by identifying the *jiva* with Brahma (Aksharbrahma), separate from its three bodies *(Nijātmānam brahmarupam...).*

Shriji Maharaj ordained that the Shikshapatri should be read daily by all his devotees.

36. Building Mandirs

During the last ten years of his life, Bhagwan Swaminarayan started building mandirs. His purpose in doing this was to preserve the *upasana* of God in the Sampraday. Secondly, he wished to foster the ancient Hindu tradition of building mandirs in society, which has through the millennia sustained and nourished the bhakti culture and character of the people of India.

Bhagwan Swaminarayan built six grand mandirs through the labour of love and devotion of his *paramhansas* and devotees. On many occasions he, too, joined in the mandir construction and supervision of work. During the construction of the mandir in Vartal, Maharaj used to sit and observe the quality of bricks that were being made at the brick-kiln. Once he picked up a few bricks and started carrying them towards the mandir site. When Nityanand Swami and Brahmanand Swami requested Maharaj to give them a few bricks, Maharaj gave them one each and carried the rest himself. Shriji Maharaj also used to remain present at the construction site of Gadhada mandir, overseeing the work done by his *paramhansas* and devotees. He had instructed all the sadhus and devotees to carry stones for the mandir on returning from the banks of the river Ghela. He himself also carried stones on his head to the site. Once, when the sadhus and devotees requested him to give the stone to them, Maharaj replied that he wished to offer his services for the mandir construction himself. On many occasions he used to supply mortar and lime to the masons on site. This was a lesson for others to serve and sacrifice. Their labour of love strengthened their bonds of pride and devotion towards the mandir and the deities within them.

In a short span of seven years (1822 to 1828) Bhagwan Swaminarayan inspired and consecrated six grand, traditional mandirs at Amdavad, Bhuj, Vartal, Dholera, Junagadh and Gadhada in Gujarat. He consecrated the deities of Sanatan Dharma, and in Vartal he installed his own *murti* – Shri Harikrishna Maharaj.

On many occasions Bhagwan Swaminarayan revealed the true creed of Akshar and Purushottam – the philosophy of Bhakta-Bhagwan that is in consonance with the tradition of Sanatan Dharma. Bhagwan Swaminarayan proclaimed that Gunatitanand Swami was Akshar, his abode and choicest disciple, and the means to moksha. He also prophesied to Kashidas Mota of Bochasan that a mandir would be built in his village, wherein he would reside with his ideal devotee. In accordance to his wishes, Shastriji Maharaj, the third successor of Bhagwan Swaminarayan, built Akshar Purushottam mandirs in Bochasan, Sarangpur and Gadhada, consecrating the *murtis* of Bhagwan Swaminarayan and Gunatitanand Swami (Akshar Purushottam Maharaj). He also built two more Akshar Purushottam mandirs in Gondal and Atladra.

Through these beautiful mandirs, Bhagwan Swaminarayan revived the bhakti tradition in all its pristine glory. For generations mandirs are revered as the form of the supreme Divinity. Their ambience inspires purity of body, mind and soul. The celebration of festivals in mandirs evokes devotional joy in the hearts of people, thus invigorating and enlightening them for the realisation of the ultimate purpose of existence. The echo of spiritual discourses and devotional services at the Swaminarayan mandirs enjoin all onto the path of bettering themselves. And in times of famine and calamity, Bhagwan Swaminarayan provided food and shelter to the afflicted, with the mandir being the centre of philanthropic work.

The renowned 19th century Gujarati poet, Nanalal, son of the great poet Dalpatram, says, "Go and sit beneath the wide dome of a Swaminarayan mandir. There, you will feel the showers of coolness descending from space, the *atma* being pacified, the heart experiencing peace and the inner fires being extinguished."

37. Meeting Sir John Malcolm

In the early nineteenth century, India was under British rule. The then Governor of Bombay, Sir John Malcolm, came on an official visit to Rajkot, Gujarat. His political agent, Mr Blane, and other officials spoke about the great social work of Bhagwan Swaminarayan in Gujarat. They reported that what they had not been able to achieve through law and order, Bhagwan Swaminarayan had done so through love and divinity. Subsequently, the Governor fervently desired to meet him. He sent a letter of invitation expressing his deep wish to meet him in Rajkot. Maharaj, despite his severe illness, consented and arrived in Rajkot. On 26 February 1830 Governor Sir John Malcolm welcomed Bhagwan Swaminarayan with due honours at the residence of his acting political agent, Mr Blane. Maharaj had brought Muktanand Swami, Gopalanand Swami, Nityanand Swami, Shukmuni Swami, Dada Khachar and a few leading devotees with him.

In the private meeting a historic dialogue between Sir Malcolm and Maharaj followed.

"Through your glory and powers you have resolved the lawlessness and moral unrest that was once prevailing in Saurashtra. Thieves and hardcore criminals have been transformed into your disciples. What we have not been able to do with the sword, you have accomplished through your divine powers," said Governor Malcolm in mixed Hindi and Gujarati.

Shriji Maharaj replied, "According to the principles of our Hindu dharma the incarnation of God descends on earth to destroy evil and unrighteousness and reestablish dharma. I have reinstated Bhagvat Dharma by explaining and inspiring the principles of morality, justice and religion in people. When you have these three elements, then only can peace and harmony prevail. But on transgressing these three principles there will be no peace and righteousness in society."

Mr Blane, who knew a little Hindi, explained to Sir Malcolm whatever he had not understood.

"Where are you from? Who are your mother and father? Your caste? And why did you renounce your home?"

Shriji Maharaj answered all his questions in detail. The Governor was pleased and requested further, "I wish to understand the principles of your religion thoroughly. If you have a book in this regard then I would like to have it."

Shriji Maharaj presented the Shikshapatri to him, which the Governor took and touched it with respect on his head. "I shall peacefully read this book," he promised.

After the dialogue the Governor honoured Maharaj by performing *pujan,* and offering a garland and a shawl. He also sprayed perfume on Maharaj's clothes. Mr Malcolm also honoured all the sadhus and devotees with garlands and shawls.

Then Maharaj introduced Dada Khachar and said, "He is a dedicated devotee, and he wishes to gift you with a beautiful Kathiawadi horse."

"The Shikshapatri you have given to me is worth a thousand horses," the Governor replied. Then he turned to Dada Khachar and praised him, "You are very fortunate and blessed in having to look after and serve Bhagwan Swaminarayan in your own house." Then, Sir John Malcolm turned to Maharaj and prayed, "Bless me for the good of my country and for the good of my enemies."

Shriji Maharaj was pleased by his prayer and praised him, "We congratulate you on your intellect. One who wishes for the good of others always benefits personally. But you have wished for the good of your enemies, so, you will definitely be blessed with goodness in your life."

Then out of curiosity the Governor asked Maharaj, "How do so many of your disciples abide by your injunctions? Despite having weapons and soldiers we cannot rule and exercise control over people."

"In the Shikshapatri that I have given to you, I have prescribed all the moral rules and regulations to be followed by my disciples. They abide by them to please me and to attain moksha. So, they naturally and easily restrain themselves."

"I would like to hear a few of the rules you have written," the Governor requested.

Maharaj told Nityanand Swami to read a few verses. On hearing about the rule of not committing suicide, the Governor enquired, "Isn't it suicide for a widow to become a sati?"

"I have abolished this custom among the Rajputs and Kathis in Saurashtra. I have explained to the widows to behold God as their husband, follow dharma and engage themselves in bhajan."

Sir John Malcolm was satisfied and happy with the darshan of and dialogue with Bhagwan Swaminarayan.

The Governor finally offered his sincere appreciations to Shriji Maharaj for coming to see him in Rajkot, despite his illness.

The copy of the Shikshapatri presented to Sir John Malcolm is preserved at the Bodleian Library of Oxford University.

38. Love for Gunatitanand Swami

In 1830, Bhagwan Swaminarayan made up his mind to end his physical stay on earth. After celebrating the Fuldol festival in February, Maharaj became ill in Gadhada. He even announced that he wanted to retire from this world. The *paramhansas* and devotees were stunned and saddened by Maharaj's words. Shriji Maharaj spent his time sleeping in the Akshar Ordi all day. He lost his appetite. During his last days, he abstained from food altogether. Maharaj told Brahmanand Swami to go to Junagadh and send Gunatitanand Swami immediately. Brahmanand Swami left with a heavy, reluctant heart, knowing full well that he would not see Maharaj again. On reaching Junagadh he told Gunatitanand Swami, "Maharaj has asked that you reach Gadhada at the earliest. Therefore, do not delay your departure for one moment." Saying this Brahmanand Swami's eyes became wet with tears.

Gunatitanand Swami understood the situation and left immediately. He walked swiftly, neither stopping along the way nor sleeping for the night. He reached Gadhada the following day. It was 28 May 1830 (A.S. 1886, Jeth *sud* 6). The entire *darbar* of Dada Khachar was plunged in silence and sadness. Whoever Swami met along his way to the Akshar Ordi were serious and silent. Their eyes were red and their hearts heavy with grief. Gunatitanand Swami understood the graveness of Maharaj's illness. When he came to Akshar Ordi, Sura Khachar informed Maharaj of Gunatitanand Swami's arrival. On hearing of Swami's name Maharaj got up from his bed with joy. "Allow him to come in immediately," Maharaj told the attendant.

Gunatitanand Swami entered the Akshar Ordi, offered his prostrations and bowed at Maharaj's feet. Tears flowed from Swami's eyes when he saw the withered face and body of Maharaj. He stood there speechless. Maharaj told everyone to leave except Swami and Mulji Brahmachari. Shriji Maharaj lovingly placed his hand on Swami and said, "Swami, you have arrived. Did I not tell you that I will call you in my last days." Both Maharaj and Swami looked at each other's eyes for some-time. Though they were in eternal communion with each other, there was sadness and pain in Swami's heart. Maharaj perceived this and said gently, "Swami! I am not separate from you." Then he added,

"Mithā vahālā kem visaru māru tamthi bāndhel tan ho,

tarasyā ne jem pānidu vahālu, bhukhyā ne bhojan ho."

"Why do you forget that you are my body.

You are dear to me as water is to one who is thirsty, and food to one who is hungry."

Shriji Maharaj beamed with joy on meeting Gunatitanand Swami. He took a little food after four days, and gave the *prasad* to Gunatitanand Swami. The *paramhansas* and devotees sighed with relief. They were happy that after so long Maharaj had at last spoken with joy and eaten something. But Maharaj had firmly decided to conclude his physical stay on earth.

Shriji Maharaj commanded the *paramhansas* and devotees who would be unable to bear his departure to go to Gujarat. Then Gopalanand Swami suggested that he send Gunatitanand Swami back to Junagadh, because he, too, would not be able to bear the pain of his demise. Maharaj smiled and replied, "Swami, Gunatitanand Swami is my Akshardham. He is divine and forever in communion with me. How can I distance him from me! Where he is, there I am, and where I am, there he is. How can he be separated from me?"

Gopalanand Swami realised the glory of Gunatitanand Swami and understood that Maharaj would continue his presence through him.

Maharaj then called the other senior sadhus and devotees inside his room. He spoke solemnly, "I have now decided to return to my abode. I will not change my resolve. So I ask you all to have forbearance. No one should commit suicide after my departure. If anyone disobeys me then he will not be blessed with Akshardham."

Shriji Maharaj's words further deepened the sadness of his disciples. Someone broke down in sobs. Maharaj calmed him and said, "There is no need to cry. God never leaves this earth. He departs from here and manifests in another form. If one does not recognise that form then I am present in the *murti*. If you offer worship to the *murti* with loving devotion then you will recognise my manifest form on earth."

Shriji Maharaj consoled his disciples, but they could not reconcile themselves with his decision to conclude his physical existence. Maharaj said, "Today is the ninth day of the bright half month. Tomorrow I shall depart." On hearing this, Dada Khachar, Jivuba, Laduba, Mulji Brahmachari and others wailed and collapsed to the ground. When they shortly came around, Maharaj beckoned everyone to leave.

On the day of his demise Maharaj called Gunatitanand Swami. "Now I shall not stay any longer in this world. You will have to spread my glory. Through your association redeem all and make them eligible to attain Akshardham. Through you everyone will experience my divine happiness. Now happily allow me to depart."

In his final moments Shriji Maharaj called for Gopalanand Swami, Muktanand Swami, Nityanand Swami, Shukanand Swami and senior sadhus and devotees. It was twelve noon. Maharaj sat up on his bed with the help of his attendants. He said his final 'Jai Swaminarayan' and sat on a seat of *darbh* grass facing east. Everyone had their eyes focused on Maharaj. Then, on 1 June 1830 (A.S. 1886, Jeth *sud* 10), through his divine powers he left his physical body and concluded his stay on earth in flesh and blood. The silence was broken by wails from all corners of the *darbar.*

The physical body of Shriji Maharaj was brought for the final rites to Lakshmi Vadi. It was placed on a pyre and after completing the final rituals, consigned to flames.

There is a memorial mandir today in his honour at Lakshmi Vadi.

Bhagwan Swaminarayan has revealed in his spiritual discourse, compiled as the Vachanamrut, that God is always present on earth through his Gunatit Sadhu or the Satpurush. He has profusely stated the glory of the Satpurush and the need for his grace to attain final liberation. Gunatitanand Swami was his choicest disciple and abode, Akshardham. He continued Maharaj's mission of redeeming people, spreading the glory of Sanatan Dharma and serving society.

39. The Eternal Bond

After the crematory rites were over at Lakshmi Vadi, everyone went to a nearby well for the ritual bath. Gunatitanand Swami saw a channel of water in the farm nourishing the tender green grass. Immediately a thought crossed his mind, "Water is the life of this grass. Oh how the grass wades in the stream! Our life was Maharaj, and he has gone!" Immediately thereafter Gunatitanand Swami lost consciousness and fell down by the channel of water. Shriji Maharaj appeared in a divine form, awakened him and said, "Swami, have I gone away? I am forever manifest in you." Then Maharaj lovingly embraced Gunatitanand Swami and thus revealed his manifestation on earth. After Maharaj's darshan Swami regained his composure, took his bath and returned to Dada Khachar's *darbar*. As time passed, Gunatitanand Swami was revered as the abode and successor of Bhagwan Swaminarayan, and the gateway to moksha. After the demise of Gunatitanand Swami the spiritual hierarchy was continued by Bhagatji Maharaj and then by Shastriji Maharaj. In 1907, in accordance with the Vedic preachings of Bhagwan Swaminarayan, Shastriji Maharaj established the Bochasanwasi Shri Akshar Purushottam Swaminarayan Sanstha (BAPS). He built five mandirs and consecrated the *murtis* of Akshar Purushottam Maharaj in the central shrine.

In 1951, Shastriji Maharaj was succeeded by Yogiji Maharaj, who established the children and youth forums and the weekly *satsang* assemblies. He also initiated 51 educated youths into the sadhu order and spread the Satsang to East Africa and England.

In 1971, when Yogiji Maharaj passed away, he was succeeded by Pramukh Swami Maharaj. He is the fifth successor in the illustrious spiritual tradition of Bhagwan Swaminarayan. He has inspired the BAPS into a worldwide socio-spiritual organisation, personally consecrating over 640 mandirs, initiating 700 youths as sadhus and having a volunteer force of 55,000 youths. His divine humanism has provided succour to countless souls in times of natural catastrophe and need.

Pramukh Swami Maharaj has inspired national and international cultural complexes like the Swaminarayan Akshardham monuments at New Delhi and in Gandhinagar, Gujarat, and *shikharbaddh* mandirs in London, Chicago, Houston and Nairobi that epitomise the glory of Indian culture, values and principles for the uplift of mankind. His striking humility, simplicity and spiritualism have impressed many religious and national leaders. And above all, his profound experience and realisation of God is the essence of his divine lustre and success.

Appendix

Impressions of Scholars and Statesmen

Bhagwan Swaminarayan's life and work (1781-1830) have had a profound impact on countless people in India and throughout the world. His universal principles of religious faith, sterling character and selfless service to society had ushered in a moral and spiritual renaissance. His life and message have touched indigenous and foreign people from all walks of life. Many past and modern astute scholars, writers and statesmen have expressed their observations about him:

What I saw of their whole system convinced me that the Swami-Narayanis are an energetic body of men, and their sect an advancing one. Without doubt the tendency of their doctrine is towards purity of life, which is supposed to be effected by suppression of the passions (*udasa*), and complete devotion to the Supreme Being. In an honest desire to purify the Vaishnava faith, this sect has done and is doing much good.

Sir Monier Williams,
Boden Professor of Sanskrit, Oxford.
Brahmanism and Hinduism or Religious Thought and Life in India

In spite of his considerable indebtedness to western thought and method, Mahatma Gandhi is perhaps most influenced in his inner-most being by the teachings of orthodox Hinduism in general, and by the teachings and activities of the Swaminarayan Sampraday above all… The contact of his early life with the Vallabhi Sampradaya has left its effect on him, yet most of his thought, activities and even methods of most of the institutions which he has been building up and serving, have the flavour of Swaminarayanism, more than that of any other sect of Hinduism.

N.A. Thoothi,
Gujarati Author.
The Vaishnavas of Gujarat

What did Swaminarayan do? The answer to this historic question in one line is: Shriji Maharaj cleansed Gujarat with the waters of Saryu and soaked it with divinity. Bhagwan Swaminarayan was the dawning sun of a new era.

Kavishwar Nanalal,
Renowned 19th century poet of Gujarat.

What Sahajanand Swami achieved in Gujarat even the political masters could not do and will not be able to.

Mahatma Gandhi

Sahajanand Swami arrested the irregularities of caste and Dharma from society and propagated the precepts of knowledge and morality. He stopped sinful behaviour and suffering. His efforts uplifted the lower classes of Gujarat. Being a Brahmin, a versatile pundit, a staunch Vaishnav and an ideal Sannyasin, by his life and work he consolidated the salient features of Gujarat's culture. A representative of a lofty bygone era, he appeared on the threshold of the nineteenth century.

K.M. Munshi,
Renowned legislator, historian,
thinker and writer of Gujarat.
Gujaratni Asmita

At a time when Gujarat-Kathiwad was steeped in darkness, with his power, Sahajanand Swami: enlightened infinite hearts, inspired thousands to sacrifice themselves on His commands, subjugated the looting instincts of scores of Kathis and Kolis, reestablished the extinct Brahmacharya ashram, enlightened the renunciant order which had become uncontrolled and wanton, laid down the ideals of self-control for the gurus and acharyas who had lapsed, gave women a well defined status in society and Sampraday, thus uplifting them,... If incarnations do occur on earth, then he can without doubt, be given the title of Avatar.

Kishorelal Mashruwala,
Eminent Gandhian thinker.
Swami Sahajanand or Swaminarayan Sampraday

But the genius of Sahajanand Swami (Swaminarayan) was not confined simply to the rigid re-establishment of Hindu worship in virgin integrity – it was also directed against the irregularities of the age and to the recovery of thousands of those unfortunate men to be found throughout Gujarat, whose means of subsistence hitherto were equally lawless and precarious: of his success in this latter respect there is abundant testimony, from the vast hordes who have been reclaimed to honest and industrious pursuits – while the present undisturbed state of the country compared to its condition previously, will speak volumes for him…

Henry George Briggs,
British Observer.
Cities of Gujarashtra

Yet his message had a revolutionary effect on the personal lives and character of thousands of people in a very lawless period: Members of martial and criminal tribes gave up meat and drink; they renounced the use of opium and tobacco, to both of which most of them were very much addicted.

Pryns Hopkins,
British Author,
Character and Personality
Vol. III No. 1, Sept. 1939

If Sahajanand Swami had not been we would not see the 'proud' Gujarat we speak of. The morality we see in Gujarat would have otherwise been an unseeable rot. Today our hearts celebrate at the name of Gujarat, but if Sahajanand Swami had not been we would have looked down in shame. Sahajanand Swami's contribution for the morality, non-violence and virtues of Gujarat is of no ordinary measure. We, the people of Gujarat, bow to Sahajanand Swami who redeemed Gujarat from its lowly state.

Chandravadan Mehta
Renowned scholar of Gujarat.

Glossary

adharma	unrighteousness, evil
akshar mukta	a jiva that has attained ultimate liberation and resides forever in Akshardham – abode of Bhagwan Swaminarayan – with a divine body
alap	a tune sung prior to or during a bhajan
anirdesh	not pointable; Akshardham
antahkaran	inner seat of thought and feeling comprising of mind, intellect, consciousness and ego
arti	Hindu ritual of waving lighted wicks before the murti of God as an act of worship
asan	Third of the eight steps of *ashtang yoga,* entailing physical exercises of postures for soundness of body, which promotes concentration
asat	opposite of *sat.* Transient, i.e., perishable, changing and bound by the constraints of time
ashtang yoga	System of Yoga comprising eight progressive steps leading ultimately to yoga, i.e., union with God. The eight steps are: *yam* (restraint), *niyam* (observance), *asan* (seat or posture), pranayam (mastering the *prans*), *pratyahar* (withdrawal), *dharna* (concentration), dhyan and samadhi
atma	The pure *jiva,* distinct from the physical, subtle and causal bodies – i.e., distinct from the *indriyas,* the *antahkaran,* worldly desires, or any other traces of *maya*
	Generally, that which pervades, inspires and governs. Thus, also refers to God as the pervader, inspirer and governor of the physical and non-physical world, i.e., *shariri*
Bhagvati diksha	initiation into the monastic order where a youth is given saffron robes to wear
brahmachari	celibate
brahmacharya	celibacy
chandlo	small, round mark – usually of kumkum or sandalwood paste – applied in the centre of the forehead indicating one's Hindu affiliation

dakshina	donation given to Brahmins at the end of a religious ceremony
darbar	court of residence belonging to a king or feudal ruler, traditionally with a central courtyard surrounded by rooms with verandas
darbh	kind of sacred grass
dharna	concentration. Sixth of the eight steps of *ashtang* yoga, entailing focusing of the mind to guide the flow of consciousness
diksha	initiation
dudhpiti	drowning of female baby in a bowl of milk
ekantik dharma	collective term for the four endeavours of dharma (religious disciplines and duties, i.e., *niyams*), *gnan* (spiritual knowledge), *vairagya* (an aversion for worldly pleasures), and bhakti (devotion) coupled with the knowledge of God's greatness – the cultivating of which will lead one to become an ekantik bhakta who transcends God's maya and attains His abode
gnan	spiritual knowledge leading to enlightenment. In particular, the knowledge of one's *atma* and the form and greatness of God
guna	quality. Principle quality of Prakruti, or maya. There are three in total: *sattvagun* ('goodness', i.e., awareness), *rajogun* ('passion', i.e., desires) and *tamogun* ('darkness', i.e., unawareness, lethargy). All beings are affected by the influence of one or a combination of these three *gunas* of maya until they become gunatit. With respect to the influence of the gunas on *jivas* and *ishwars,* the *gunas* elicit in people's minds three different types of moods as follows: a person in *sattvagun* is calm, placid, peaceful; a person in *rajogun* is desirous, active, sensual; a person in *tamogun* is volatile, lethargic, drowsy
gunatit	one who is above the three *gunas* of *rajas, tamas* and *sattva*; above maya
hindolo	swing
indriya	sense, through which one can 'know' and perform actions

ishwar	one of the five eternal entities. Infinite in number. Similar to *jiva* with respect to being bound by maya – i.e., composed of the 24 elements, having three bodies, three states, three *gunas,* desires, etc. – but involved in the processes and lordship of the universes, and thus endowed by God with greater powers. Brahmā, Vishnu, Shiv and all entities greater than them upwards to Prakruti-Purush, are considered *ishwars*
janoi	sacred thread
jiva	soul bound to mundane desires
kanthi	double-threaded necklace, usually made of small tulsi beads, received by *satsangis* upon initiation into the Satsang Fellowship, and worn as a sign of their affiliation to Bhagwan Swaminarayan. Derived from noun 'kantha', meaning neck
mahamantra	great mantra
mala	rosary
maya	one of the five eternal realities; ignorance, darkness, material universe
moksha	liberation; deliverance of the *jiva* from recurring births and deaths
mukta	a liberated soul. A resident of any abode of God who has been freed from a lower plane of existence to a more spiritually elevated state. There are varying levels of spiritual elevation, i.e., muktas of Badrikashram, Shwetdwip, Golok, etc. The highest level of *mukta, akshar-mukta,* has attained ultimate liberation and is free from the bondage of maya and the consequent cycle of births and deaths
murti	sacred idol of God that is revered and worshipped
nirdesh	pointable
niyam	Second step of *ashtang* yoga, entailing observance of religious practices and code of dharma for the control and refinement of the mind
paramhansa	supreme swan. A male sadhu of the highest order, characterised by his ability to discriminate

between *sat* and *asat* – just as swans were traditionally considered to be able to distinguish between milk mixed with water. Traditionally, they renounce not only worldly pursuits but also all religious accessories such as rites, symbols and objects – daily worship, *chandlo, kanthi,* etc. – and lead a life of traveling and preaching. In the time of Bhagwan Swaminarayan, there was an illustrious legion of 3,000 learned, talented and saintly sadhus of which 500 were initiated into the *paramhansa* order. These were later re-initiated as sadhus and had returned to performing all traditional religious rites and rituals, but were still known as *paramhansas*

pran	vital airs, derived from verb-root 'pran'– to breathe. Collective term referring to the principle life force or energy flowing within the primary life-currents of the body, called *vayus,* which control crucial bodily functions. There are five main *vayus:* (1) *pran* – exhaled breath (2) *apan* – inhaled breath (3) *saman* – equalising breath (4) *udan* – ascending breath (5) *vyan* – retrained breath and five subordinate *vayus:* (1) nag, (2) kurma, (3) kukal, (4) devadatta, and (5) dhananjay
pranam	obeisance offered with folded hands
prasad	sanctified food, blessed and consecrated by having been offered to God
pujan	the act of worshipping
rag	tune, mode of music
rajas	one of the three *gunas,* attribute/state of: activity, restlessness, anger, violence, desire to satisfy the indriyas and extravagance
rajogun	quality of passion
ras	circular traditional dance accompanied by devotional singing
rotla	a basic unleavened bread-like staple food of many parts of Gujarat, made generally of millet flour that is kneaded and patted into a flat, circular shape before being cooked on an earthen or metal hot plate
sadguru	a high ranking sadhu, also a realised sadhu

sat	permanent, i.e., imperishable and unchanging. Transcending time, and thus unbound by the past, the present and the future
satsang	the practice of spiritually associating with the Satpurush, fellow *satsangis,* one's own *atma* and the sacred scriptures of the Satsang fellowship
satsangi	one who practices *satsang*
sattva	second of the three *gunas,* attribute of: clarity and purity of thought, excellence, mental poise
sattvagun	quality of goodness
sharir	embodiment. Generally, that which is pervaded, inspired and governed by the *atma*. Refers to the physical and non-physical world, which is pervaded, inspired and governed by God, its *shariri*
shariri	that which is embodied. Generally, that which pervades, inspires and governs the *sharir*. Refers to God as the pervader, inspirer and governor of the physical and non-physical world, His *sharir*
shikharbaddh	mandir in which five *artis* are performed daily and daily worship of the deities is performed by sadhus
sud	bright half of lunar month
sukhdi	a sweet delicacy of wheat flour, ghee and gur
tamas	part of maya. Tamogun is the attribute of inactivity, lethargy and darkness
tamogun	quality of darkness
tilak	'U' shaped mark made with sandalwood paste on one's forehead, chest and arms
tilak-chandlo	'U' shaped mark made with sandalwood paste and a round mark of kumkum in its centre; a hallmark of one's allegiance to the Swaminarayan Sampraday
trishul	trident
upasana	philosophical understanding of the nature of God as well as the mode of worship of God, i.e., how one understands God's nature, and how one worships Him. Sometimes synonymous with bhakti
vad	dark half of lunar month

vairagya	detachment. An aversion or strong, persistent dislike, generally for the world and worldly pleasures. Characterised by remaining detached from the body and the world
Vashishta Smruti	a scripture
yagna	sacrificial worship. Ceremonial ritual performed as a form of worship to seek the good favour and receive the blessings of the deities
yagna kund	square mouthed pit or container used for offerings to the fire placed in it
Yagnavalkya Smruti	one of the principal ancient Smruti scriptures, second in authority only to the earlier Manu Smruti dealing with moral codes. Ascribed to Yagnavalkya Rishi. One of the eight scriptures accepted as authoritative by Bhagwan Swaminarayan
yam	restraint, derived from the verb-root 'yam' – to restrain. First of the eight steps of *ashtang* yoga, entailing virtuous and moral living for purity of mind and unobstructed concentration